Amigurumi

Amigurumi

**Make 15 crocheted toys
and learn how to design
hundreds more**

Annie Obaachan

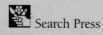

Search Press

This edition published in 2008 by
Search Press Ltd
Wellwood
North Farm Road
Tunbridge Wells
Kent TN2 3DR
www.searchpress.com

This book was designed and produced by
Quintet Publishing Limited, 6 Blundell Street, London N7 9BH, UK

Art Director: Sofia Henry
Designer: Jason Anscomb
Photography: Lizzie Orme
Illustrator: Bernard Chau
Project Editor: Katy Bevan
Managing Editor: Donna Gregory
Publisher: Gillian Laskier

Printed in China

ISBN: 978-1-84448-309-9
QTT.CTO

10 9 8 7 6 5 4 3 2 1

Contents

Foreword

My mother taught me to crochet when I was quite small. I failed the first time round and didn't enjoy it, but when I started again as a teenager it all came back to me. I remember well the crochet bikini I made out of fluorescent-pink-itchy yarn.

In Japan the third of March is the Doll's Festival. Each family has a set of dolls that were bought, or handed down the generations. When I was born my grandmother bought a set for me, to celebrate being the first girl born to the family. I had a collection of regular children's dolls as well – Snoopy, giant bears, and the like. I also had some kokeshi dolls as souvenirs from different parts of the country – although the stories we learned about them still give me goose bumps as kokeshi means, "disappeared child." A long time ago when Japan was a rural community, farmers in the countryside were often struggling. People had to sell or sacrifice their children to give their spirits to their god, so the wooden kokeshi dolls were a child-replacement.

I studied fashion design at the Bunka Fashion College, Tokyo. There I learned skills from pattern cutting and sewing to merchandising. Then

Annie Obaachan

(Grannie Annie)

later I worked for the costume studio at Disneyland making life-sized outfits. I made a flesh-coloured body suit with muscle textures for a sailor, and plenty of mermaids' tails, that kind of silly thing.

I was dreaming about coming to London, and saving money for the trip. When I finally got to London I met Rosie and Harriet from Tatty Devine. They introduced me to Rachael Matthews and the Cast Off knitting group. I then helped Rachael with Cast Off, working on her books *Knitorama* and *Hookorama*, before helping with her exhibition in 2006.

I love to crochet anything. My ambition is to make a range of crocheted-popcorn jewellery... coming soon!

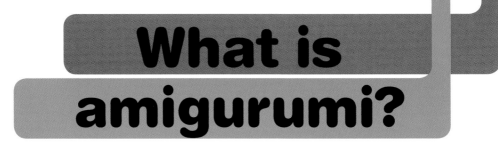

What is amigurumi?

TELL YOUR FRIENDS YOU HAVE A BOOK ON "AMIGURUMI", AND YOU'LL FIND IT IS A LOVELY WORD TO SAY.

You can use your whole mouth to form the word, in a variety of different voices... Aa-miii-gaa-ruu-miii. The word has so many vowel sounds, that you can pull up to five funny faces just in the process of saying it. Once you have practised saying "amigurumi" in an animated manner, and learned the basics of crochet, you have probably grasped the concept of this book. You are about to launch yourself into a cartoon world, where any mood is acceptable.

Amigurumi is a recently coined word. "Ami" means knit in Japanese, and "nuigurumi" means stuffed creature – so knit it, stuff it and you have amigurumi. These are anthropomorphic creatures that you are giving life to – you could never make the same one twice, as each one is unique.

Japan has a rich history of textiles, especially in the art of kimonos, where you find beautifully crafted *ikat-kasuri* weaving, batik, *shibori*, wood-block printing, to name but a few – but no knitting. Knitting and crochet are not indigenous to Japan. The samurai warriors took up knitting to make socks with toes that allowed more freedom of motion, but for a long time, they were the only ones forming knitting circles.

In the West, we have no history of amigurumi as we see it in this book. We talk about yarn, and immediately think of functional items, like cardigans, jumpers, socks and gloves. Traditionally, we knit or crochet from patterns, typed in an abbreviated language, which instructs us to make shapes that we join, and fashion around our bodies. Without a picture of one that's been made earlier, when we read our patterns, we can only imagine the finished result.

The Japanese, with no prior knitting tradition, invented a new use for knitting and crochet in their culture and a new way of writing patterns. Amigurumi seems to have grown naturally with the way the charts developed. Pictures are drawn with crochet and sometimes the images become little creatures. Japanese writing comprises pictures and symbols, and knitting and crochet stitches are represented in the same

way. Throughout this book, you will see beautifully drawn charts. Don't feel you have to "read" every stitch. Charts are designed as a full picture of how a pattern is expected to evolve. They show you where you are heading. Let your eyes roll around and around the spiralled paths and kaleidoscopic circles, and they will take you on a rhythmic journey towards finding a new friend. Meditating in circles and lines gives us plenty of time to conjure up extraordinary personae. The Japanese would never waste time telling you how to knit. They assume that you know the basics, and expect you to dive in and make whatever comes naturally.

So why do we want to make little stuffed crochet creatures in the first place? They may be very small and cute, but they have weighty cultural significance. Type amigurumi in a search engine, and they are everywhere, millions of them, and some of them are real enough to write their own blogs. Amigurumi as a phenomenon has been growing slowly since the 1950s. It was at this time that Japanese culture moved towards cuteness, or *kawaii*, inventing characters like Hello Kitty, a cute white kitten with a little bow on one ear, who could be happy or sad, but we're not sure which because she has no mouth and just stares. At the end of World War II, atom bombs were dropped on Hiroshima and Nagasaki. Japan lost its political strength, and its ancient culture, leaving behind a country like a lost child, to be re-born, and re-formed with a deliberate avoidance of what had happened before. It was not possible to think about what had happened. A new culture of "cuteness" served as a mask for all the atrocities.

During the 1960s, the Japanese government encouraged economic expansion over cultural preservation, dissolving communities and regionally distinct traditions. Families moved to big cities to find jobs. Little Hello Kitty and her other nu-cultural friends were developed as mass marketable icons, spreading a cute, pacifying force over a new nation of "salary men" and "office ladies". These were white-collar workers, who turned Japan around into an economic power. These slaves to the wage, with long working hours and a low prestige in the corporate hierarchy, were the workers that helped develop technology we now use worldwide. Another new word was born – *karoshi* – meaning death from overwork.

Most of us have a friend, or are ourselves, an absentee who is devoted to their work and missing out on the rest of life. A typical modern job might demand the wearing of a uniform, and the conducting of friendships through text messaging and email, which unfortunately means we can't use all the little noises, faces and gestures we normally use to express ourselves. Amigurumi step into the breach. They offer us cute individual characters formed by human hands. The materials are chosen with love and care. The pacifying force is still there but it's heavily personalized. They are sweet gestures, with no particular depth of message, but characters with very colourful, anthropological histories, which are a light relief in a time when collective joy and culture can be of second importance.

There might be someone over there, sitting at their desk, on the end of a mass of electrical connections, whose life would be greatly enriched by a couple of fire-fighter pigs, which don't quite look like the ones demonstrated on page 46 of this book, because you made them yourself and they have become their own characters. In addition, if you are one of those workers who is an integral part of a larger machine, and you never see the product of what your company makes, then crafting an amigurumi superhero panda to decorate your office is a fast route to satisfaction. On the other hand, maybe something shocked you and you don't know what to say or do. You might need space to organize your thoughts, but in the meantime, making little magpies sitting on a washing line might make you feel better.

Rachael Matthews

We are free to go forth and crochet. You can grunt, growl or make cute little baby noises while your hands are working on the lovely projects in the pages that follow. As the faces start to emerge and smile back, you are in this together. Soon you will find a completely new species staring back at you, asking you to join them.

Japanese dolls

There is a long history of doll making in Japan, which runs parallel to the culture of giving gifts, or *omiyage*. Giving gifts at every opportunity, to a new colleague, neighbour, or just as a token of friendship, is a way of life in Japan. Dolls from different regions became suitable gifts or souvenirs for bringing home after a trip, as symbols of purity or as good luck charms.

Kokeshi are traditional dolls originating from northern Japan. They have no arms or legs, just a simple torso and oversized head. Usually carved in wood, the designs vary depending on the region. Dolls that are more creative, with expressions and fashionable dress, are now in vogue. **Momiji** dolls are a modern version of these gifts of friendship, which have a hole in the base where you can insert a small note to the recipient, and have become collectible items.

Daruma dolls are representations of a Buddhist priest, Bodhidharma. The dolls have no arms and legs, resembling a large head. They are usually made of papier mâché and painted red. Given as gifts at New Year, you paint in one eye to represent making a resolution, then, when the challenge is achieved, you can paint in the other. These days they are available to bulk-buy as corporate gifts.

Okiagari-koboshi are much like the daruma dolls, but blue and white. They too represent a priest, and have a rotund shape. The weighted base means that they bounce back upright when knocked down, like a child's toy. They symbolize the resilience needed to bounce back from the challenges that life throws at us.

Hakata dolls are carved from clay, then a mould is made to cast a finer doll. It is thought that hakata were originated by a master tile-maker working to build Fukuoka Castle in the seventeenth century. Pottery became fashionable and the dolls' popularity spread across the country.

Hina Matsuri, or the Doll's Festival, is celebrated in the spring. Traditionally set adrift in a river, these beautiful handmade dolls now tend to be saved, and collected from one year to the next. Originally made from a clay-like sawdust paste, and painted with powdered seashell and animal glue (*gofun*), they were dressed in traditional costumes. Bought now, they are more likely to be mass-produced.

Traditional Japanese dolls are collector's items. Left: these wooden kokeshi in Sakunami-style are from the Sendai area. Right: a daruma stares blankly, waiting for his eyes to be painted in.

Amigurumi

Making crochet dolls

Crafted with circular crochet, amigurumi differ only slightly from other crocheted items. They are often worked in spirals, rather than in steps – if you wanted to keep stripes level, without creating a step, you would make an elevating chain at the beginning of each row. Spirals are much easier, as you just keep on going without even linking the rows with a slip stitch. This will be easier for newcomers, as anyone who has been doing crochet for a while will be stuck with the turning-chain habit. You can use either technique with the patterns in this book.

Made using a hook slightly smaller than you would normally use for the weight of yarn, amigurumi can have a very tight gauge. This is good, as the stuffing will not fall out through any holes in the firm fabric. Experiment using different yarns. Fluffy mohair and alpaca yarns are ideal for some of the more hairy creatures, as well as being comforting and soft to hold. Acrylic and woolen yarns have good elasticity, while pure cotton yarns will help you to keep a tight tension as it has very little "give".

For stuffing your creations, the material that you use depends on the size of the creature, the desired effect, and most importantly, what you have on hand. Toy stuffing like polyester, or cotton wadding, is probably the most used item. However, if you don't have any, and you are in a hurry, you can cut up old, or laddered tights. If the critter is really tiny, you may be able to make do with scraps of yarn.

Plastic pellets are useful for keeping the bottom of the shape heavy, making your figure more stable and able to stand up easily. Use pellets in the bottom half of the stuffing, in the feet or tail, then continue with soft stuffing for the rest of the body. Stuffing completely with pellets will create a bean bag effect, where the beans move around the body.

HOW TO READ A CHART

In Japan, they just use charts. This is also true in continental European countries like France and Spain. In the USA, and the traditional UK, we like to have it written out. So, for those of you not used to using a chart, prepare to be amazed. It makes the whole thing much easier. You can visualize the shape you are going to make before it happens, which seems, logically, to be a better way to get the information into your brain and out through your hands.

These charts are simplicity itself, as they mostly use only one type of stitch. Follow a circular chart from the centre. The loops will indicate the beginning of each row, so you can keep count (it may be useful to use a stitch marker, or ring of scrap yarn as well). Each X is one crochet stitch, and where there is an arrow, it means that this is an increase or decrease, depending on which way the arrow is pointing. It should be obvious; if you are getting bigger, it means increasing. The charts change to straight lines to show the shape getting smaller again – then the decreases are easier to see. (See the symbol chart on page 29.)

Materials

HOOKS

Crochet hooks come in all shapes and sizes. In fact, even some that are the same size will say something different on them, just to confuse you. The US has its own system. In Europe, the sizes are measured in millimetres.

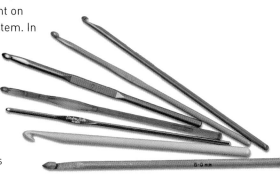

There are also traditional sizing systems in the UK, Canada and Japan, so if you inherit vintage hooks you should size them with a gauge, or check the conversion charts on page 21. Carved from wood, bone or ivory, older hooks sometimes have hooks at both ends. You can find some early Bakelite and resin hooks in antique shops, although they are increasingly sought after by collectors.

Used for the finest crochet work, fine steel hooks or pins work well with shiny, mercerised cotton or silks. Chunky and novelty yarns can be worked with giant plastic hooks. Hooks made of the finest woods, or bamboo, are beautiful to handle, although many hookers prefer the speed of an aluminium hook with a soft and ergonomic grip.

YARNS

You can crochet with any kind of long thread, but the best results are often obtained with smooth, well-spun yarns. Any yarn that could split, will split when you try to crochet with it. The joy of making small things is that you get to use up all those scraps of yarn that have been left over from other projects. We don't specify the brands of yarn used in this book. Some of them were scraps from the bottom of a workbox, others were expensive alpacas. The point is you can use what you have, thus making your critters unique, as well as saving pennies.

Best kept tied to your workbasket: sharp scissors for cutting yarn and trimming ends.

Knitters' pins with large heads are useful for pinning together shapes.

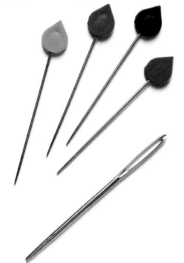

You'll need a blunt-ended needle for sewing up seams and threading in ends. [as above]

Split stitch markers are good for crochet, so that you can mark the beginning of each round.

A tape measure is good to check the tension, if you have been given one, or if you want to repeat a shape in different yarns.

Reading patterns

Looking at a crochet pattern for the first time must feel like reading another language. The shortened words are there to prevent laborious repetition and to make the patterns shorter and easier to follow. If in doubt, look at the abbreviations chart below to clarify what is meant.

CROCHET ABBREVIATIONS	
*	repeat instructions between asterisks as many times as directed or repeat from a given set of instructions
alt	alternate
approx	approximately
beg	begin/beginning
bet	between
ch	chain stitch
cm	centimetre(s)
col	colour
cont	continue
dc	double crochet
dc2tog	double crochet 2 stitches together
dtr	double treble crochet
dec	decrease/decreases/decreasing
foll	follow/follows/following
inc	increase/increases/increasing
mm	millimetre(s)
rep	repeat(s)
rnd(s)	round(s)
RS	right side
dc2tog	double crochet 2 stitches together
sk	skip/miss
ss	slip stitch
st(s)	stitch(es)
tog	together
tr	treble crochet
yoh	yarn over hook

US CROCHET TERMS ARE DIFFERENT		
US	**UK**	
Sl st	ss	slip stitch
ch	ch	chain
sc	dc	US single crochet = UK double crochet
dc	tr	US double crochet = UK treble crochet
tr	dtr	US treble crochet = UK double treble crochet
dtr	trtr	US double treble crochet = UK triple treble crochet

Welcome to the kooky world of hook sizes. The letters and numbers may vary, so if in doubt, and you probably will be, the metric sizes are the only ones that you can check with a tape measure. Your knitting needle gauge will also work for the metric sizes so you can convert those lovely vintage patterns. Beware though, Japanese hook sizes are different again. They start off looking similar to the American sizes, then vary, then after 7mm they revert to the metric system. Good luck!

Old UK	Metric	USA	Japanese
14	2 mm		0
	2.25 mm	B-1	
12	2.5 mm		1 (2.4 mm)
	2.75 mm	C-2	2 (2.7 mm)
11	3 mm		3
10	3.25 mm	D-3	4 (3.4 mm)
9	3.5 mm	E-4	5 (3.6 mm)
	3.75 mm	F-5	6 (3.9 mm)
8	4 mm	G-6	7 (4.2 mm)
7	4.5 mm	7	8
6	5 mm	H-8	9 (4.8 mm)
			10 (5.1 mm)
5	5.5 mm	I-9	11 (5.4 mm)
4	6 mm	J-10	13
3	6.5 mm	K-10½	14 (6.3 mm)
			15 (6.6 mm)
2	7 mm		7 mm
0	8 mm	L-11	8 mm
00	9 mm	M/N-13	9 mm
000	10 mm	N/P-15	10 mm
	12 mm		
	15 mm	P/Q	

Crochet techniques

The basics of crochet are very simple. Once you have made a basic chain you are well on your way, as even the most complicated and decorative stitches are just variations on this simple stitch. These instructions are for a right-handed person. If you are left-handed, look at the step images in a mirror and they will show you the correct way to do the stitch.

Holding the hook and yarn

There are many individual ways of holding the hook and yarn in crochet and it may feel awkward at first. Here are just two examples – choose whichever variation seems to come naturally to you.

1. Hold the hook in your right hand as you would a knife.
2. Hold the hook in your right hand as you would a pencil.

Wrap the ball end of the yarn around the little finger of your left hand, passing it under the third or middle finger and over your forefinger, using the forefinger to create tension. OR Wrap the ball end of the yarn around the little finger of your left hand, passing it over the middle finger. Hold the work steady with your thumb and forefinger, using the middle finger to create tension.

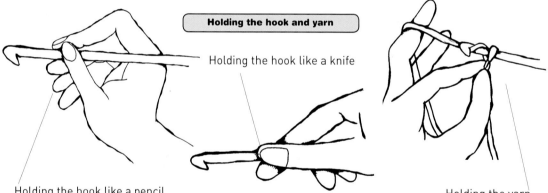

Holding the hook and yarn

Holding the hook like a knife

Holding the hook like a pencil

Holding the yarn

Make a slipknot

Make a loop in the yarn. With your crochet hook catch the ball end of the yarn and draw through loop. Pull firmly on yarn and hook to tighten knot to create your first loop.

Slipknot

Making a chain

Making a chain

1. To make a chain, hold the tail end of yarn with the left hand and bring the yarn over hook (yoh) by passing hook in front of the yarn, under and around it.
2. Keeping the tension in the yarn taut, draw the hook and yarn through the loop.
3. Pull the yarn and hook through the hole and begin again, ensuring that the stitches are fairly loose. Repeat to make the number of chain required. As the chain lengthens keep hold of the bottom edge to maintain the tension.

How to count a chain

To count the stitches, use the right side of the chain, or the side that has more visible and less twisted "V" shapes, as shown. Don't count the original slip stitch, but count each "V" as one chain.

Count a chain

Make a slip stitch (ss)

A slip stitch is used to join one stitch to another or a stitch to another point, as in joining a circle, and is usually made by picking up two strands of a stitch. However, where it is worked into the starting chain only pick up the back loop.

1. Insert the hook into the back loop of the next stitch and pass yarn over hook (yoh), as in chain stitch.
2. Draw yarn through both loops on stitch and repeat.

Working in the round

There are two ways to begin circular crochet – with a chain or a loop. Also known as a magic ring, or finger loop, a loop is the more usual way to make amigurumi. This way of working in the round ensures that there is no hole in the middle of the work, as there is with a chain ring, as the central hole is adjustable and can be pulled tightly closed.

Making a magic ring
1. Make a loop with tail end of yarn on right, ball end on left.
2. Pull ball end through loop (you will need to steady work with hand).
3. Make one chain through loop on hook you have drawn through to steady the round.
4. Work as many dc, or whatever stitch you are using, into the loop as is required by pattern.
5. Pull the ends of yarn tight to draw in circle, so you have no hole in the middle of first round.

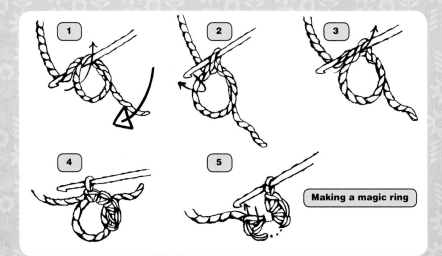

Making a magic ring

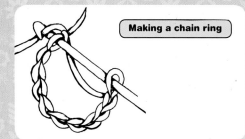

Making a chain ring

Making a chain ring
1. Work a chain as long as required by pattern.
2. Join last chain to first with a slip stitch. Begin first round by working into each chain stitch.

Double crochet (dc)

This is the main stitch that is used in amigurumi.

1. Insert hook, front to back into next stitch, two strands and one loop on hook. Yoh.
2. Draw through one loop to front, there should be two loops on hook. Yoh.
3. Draw through both loops to complete double crochet. Work one sc into every stitch to end of round.

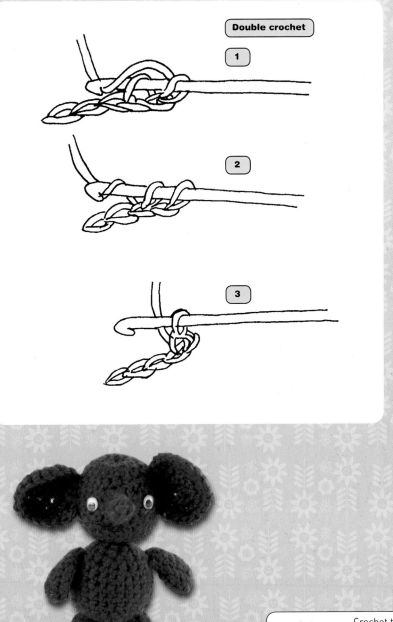

Treble crochet (tr)

This makes a more open fabric. The stitch is called a treble because of the three moves to make the stitch.

1. Wrap the yarn over the hook (yoh) from back to front. Insert hook into next stitch, from front to back. Yoh again and draw through stitch.
2. There should be three loops on hook. Yoh and pull through two loops. Two loops on hook. Yoh. Pull through remaining two loops to complete.

Half-treble crochet
The half-treble is just that, half a treble crochet. In step 2, pull through all the remaining loops in one movement.

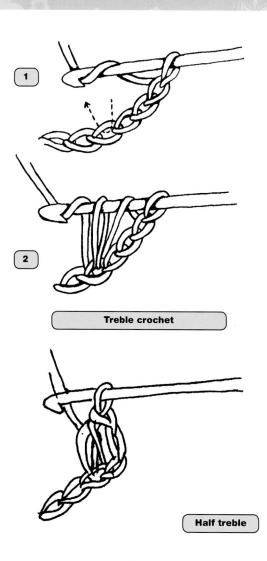

Treble crochet

Half treble

Double treble (dtr)

This elongated stitch is only used once in the wings of the magpies, so you don't have to worry about it until page 76.

1. Wrap yarn round hook twice (yoh twice). Insert hook into next stitch, yoh again.
2. Pull yarn through stitch to front, there should be four loops on hook, yoh. Draw yarn through two loops, leaving three loops on hook.
3. Yoh. Draw yarn through two loops, leaving two loops on hook, yoh.
4. Pull yarn through both remaining loops to complete double treble.

Double treble crochet

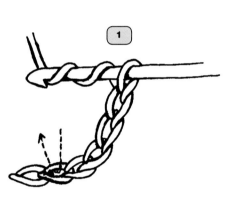

1

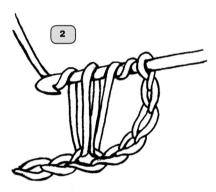

2

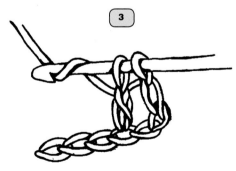

3

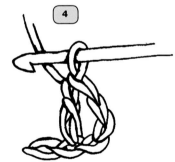

4

Putting it all together

Finishing is a very important part of crochet as it could make or break your project. The perfect join should be one you can't distinguish from the work, as bad finishing is always noticeable and messy. Luckily, most of your finishing points will be hidden in the joints of the animal, so often there is no need to even close the shape completely.

1. When you finish off the end of your arm, or leg, keep a long yarn end for sewing in, then when you are attaching the limb to the body you will be using the same colour.

2. Hold the two pieces to be connected together in your left hand, or in your right if you are left-handed. With the left-over yarn and a blunt tapestry needle sew the two pieces together with a whipstitch. Take the needle into the main body, and bring the needle back up inside the edge of the new limb. Continue all the way around.

3. As the yarn is the same colour, the stitches will be almost invisible. Piece the sections together as shown in your assembly diagram.

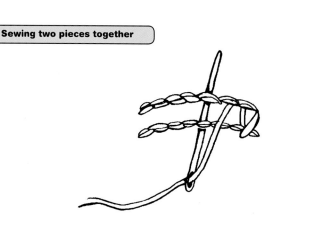

Sewing two pieces together

Fastening off

1. After finishing the last stitch, snip off yarn from ball, leaving a couple of centimetres to weave in. Yoh.
2. Draw through tail, pulling tightly to fasten.

Weaving in ends

1. Use hook to draw yarn through at least five stitches, winding the yarn over and under as you go to secure yarn and ensure it doesn't work free.
2. Snip off excess yarn.

Slip stitch join

Place two pieces together, right sides facing. Work a row of slip stitch along the join, inserting needle through back loops only of both pieces (the two loops which touch when placed side by side).

Double crochet join

Place two pieces together, right sides facing. Work a row of sc along the join of the two pieces, going through the whole of both stitches.

Whipstitch

Place two pieces together, and using a knitter's needle, join the back loops of each piece with a diagonal stitch motion. Use this stitch when attaching patches of felt, or other fabric, for faces or clothing.

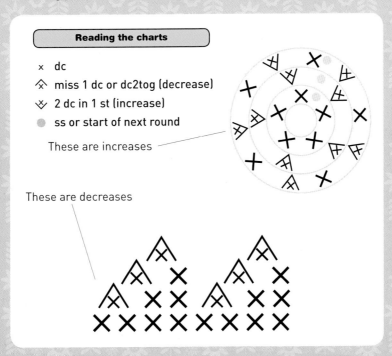

Reading the charts

×   dc

⋀   miss 1 dc or dc2tog (decrease)

⋎   2 dc in 1 st (increase)

●   ss or start of next round

These are increases

These are decreases

Design your own

Designing animals from sketches

You may be able to picture something in your imagination, but it is often only when consigning it to paper that it really begins to emerge and develop. You may notice inconsistencies in your original plan, and be able to correct them, before proceeding with any work. Patterns and shapes may emerge that were not obvious before. It is difficult for any mind to put together three-dimensional shapes without drawing them out first, and since most handicraft takes some time, it is best not to waste yours by not planning thoroughly. Don't be put off if you feel you are not a natural artist. Sketches are just that, sketchy: they are simply a tool, not the final product.

Take your inspiration from nature, sketching your pets, animals in a field or at a zoo. If working from the real thing is not an option, use photographs of animals (either your own, or from books and magazines). Use your sketching to simplify the shapes of the animal's body – perhaps the body is egg-shaped, while the head is more spherical. Once you start looking closely, you'll realize that all animals are made up of the same simple sphere, egg, cylinder or triangular shapes. You can crochet modules of different shapes and sizes (see page 36).

Consider whether your creature is on all fours, of if it will sit or stand up. Take balance into account when considering proportions – a huge head will find it hard to balance on a tiny body and legs, and likewise a tiny head will get lost on a large frame. Thinking about shape also allows you to consider which technique would be most suitable to create the effect that you need. A curled edge or striped body, for instance, may need a particular stitch.

TIP
Experimenting with different yarn weights and fibres will help you create amigurumi with an exciting range of textures, even though you only use the one crochet stitch.

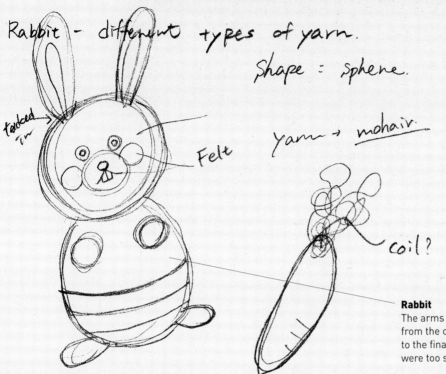

Rabbit - different types of yarn.

Shape = sphere.

tacked in →

Felt

yarn → mohair.

coil?

Rabbit
The arms and legs changed
from the original sketch
to the final version, as they
were too small.

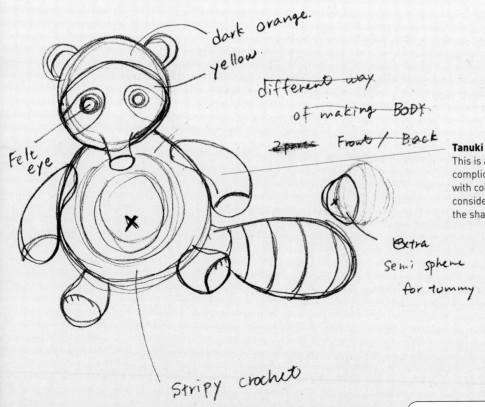

Tanuki (racoon dog). two colours crocheting.

dark orange.

yellow.

different way
of making BODY
2 parts Front / Back

Felt
eye

different way
of making BODY
Front / Back

Tanuki
This is a more
complicated design,
with colour changes to
consider, alongside
the shapes.

Extra
semi sphere
for tummy

Stripy crochet

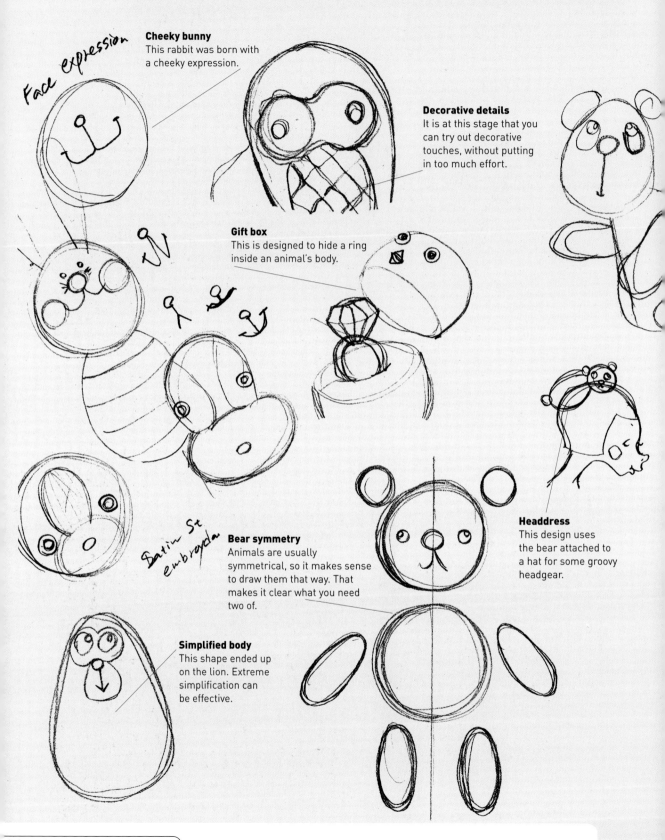

Cheeky bunny
This rabbit was born with a cheeky expression.

Decorative details
It is at this stage that you can try out decorative touches, without putting in too much effort.

Gift box
This is designed to hide a ring inside an animal's body.

Headdress
This design uses the bear attached to a hat for some groovy headgear.

Bear symmetry
Animals are usually symmetrical, so it makes sense to draw them that way. That makes it clear what you need two of.

Simplified body
This shape ended up on the lion. Extreme simplification can be effective.

Owl evolution
This lovely nocturnal
creature is actually
quite a complicated
group of shapes.

Simplified owl
This is a simplified version of
the original owl drawing.

Final shape
This is the final shape, where
the whole bird is reduced to
one main shape, and the eyes
have become exaggerated.

Lion's mane
The lion's mane becomes his
distinguishing feature.

Making shapes with circular crochet

When you've had a little experience of making amigurumi creatures, it's easy to create your own designs. Great drawing skills and knowledge of animal anatomy are not required. Working from photographic reference, heads can be simplified to spheres, bodies become simple egg shapes, and arms and legs are sausages. Look at the proportions of the animal and exaggerate these to create stylized amigurumi creatures. The majority of amigurumi seem to have distorted proportions, part of their _kawaii_ appeal. They have oversized heads and large doleful eyes.

Working in rounds, as opposed to rows, means the work continues as such, with no turning. This means it is easy to lose which row you are on and stitch markers are a good idea to remind you of where you started. Either you work in spirals, or the last stitch of each round is joined by a slip stitch to the first stitch, it doesn't matter which you choose (see page 16).

FLAT DISC

To create a flat circle, rather than a tube, you will need to increase in every row. Work two stitches into each stitch in the first row, then into every other stitch in the following row, every third stitch in the third row, and so on, until you reach the diameter you require.

SPHERE

To make a three-dimensional round shape you will need to increase the diameter, then level off briefly before beginning to decrease. Work two stitches into each stitch in the first row, then every other stitch in the following row, every third stitch in the third row. Keep straight for one round before beginning to reduce stitches. Do this by working two stitches together every alternate stitch in the following row, and every third stitch in the next row, and so on.

TO JOIN IN NEW YARN

When the yarn runs out, or you want to change colour, change yarns carefully, in order to prevent making a hole. Fasten off first colour and make a slipknot on your hook. Insert hook from front to back in stitch where you wish to begin new colour. Draw the hook through to front. Insert the hook into next stitch and work the stitch required by your pattern.

EGG SHAPE

To make the fat end of the egg, increase in every stitch in the first row, every alternate stitch in the second row, every third stitch in the third row, every forth stitch in the forth row. Keep straight for one round, then begin decreasing gradually as before, but with a straight row between each decrease row (as used in the Penguin pattern).

SAUSAGE

This is similar to making a sphere. After the initial increasing rows keep straight for the required length, then begin decreasing rows as before.

HALF SPHERE

Make this just like the sphere, but fasten off at the halfway point.

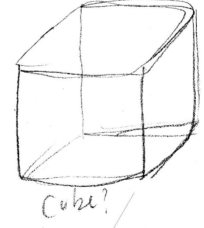

SQUARES

It can be done, but not in rounds. Don't bother, as there aren't many animals that need cubes.

Finishing touches

Embroidery is an effective way of adding interest to your projects and complements the texture of crochet. Here are some simple stitches that you may like to try. It may help to use a blunt knitter's needle, as this will not split the yarn as embroidery needles do, and will slip through the crochet stitches easily.

CHAIN STITCH

Insert needle from back to front of work and loop the thread back into same hole from front to back. Catch the loop with the point of the needle to create a chain. This is a useful stitch for curved shapes like flowers, or for handwriting script.

BLANKET STITCH

This stitch creates a neat edge, and is useful for straightening an uneven selvedge. Working along the edge, secure yarn at the back of work, insert the needle from front to back, with needle coming out of work in front of loop made by yarn. Pull needle through, tightening yarn against edge of work, repeat for length of edge.

SATIN STITCH

Work stitches closely together along the shape of the pattern you wish to make, keeping edges of shape even. This is most commonly used as a filler for eyes and other solid shapes.

OTHER EMBELLISHMENTS

Plastic eyes can give a fun look to your creations. They are available in all sorts of sizes from craft shops, or on the Internet. There are even people out there who are making their own design of eyes specially for the growing amigurumi market. When you have your correct choice of eye and the critter is near completion, glue them on with PVA glue. Some novelty yarns may resist the use of glue, so you will have to try another approach.

Felt or fabric can be used to emphasize eyes, cheeks, noses, and other facial features. Craft felt is a favourite, as it doesn't fray, so you can cut any shape and glue or stitch it on. The field mouse on page 94 has the softest felt ears. Cut the felt to shape, then stitch around using a plain or decorative stitch. Blanket stitch would work well here.

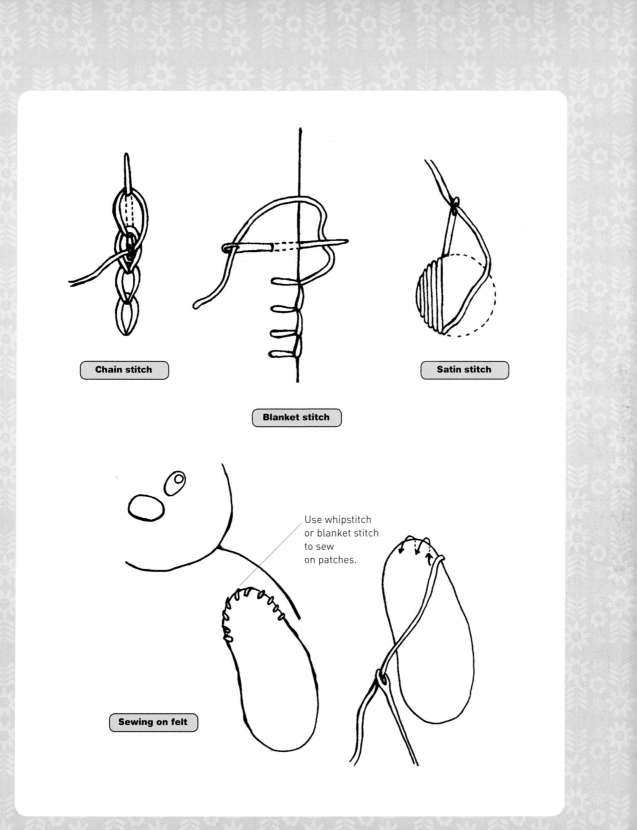

Chain stitch

Blanket stitch

Satin stitch

Use whipstitch
or blanket stitch
to sew
on patches.

Sewing on felt

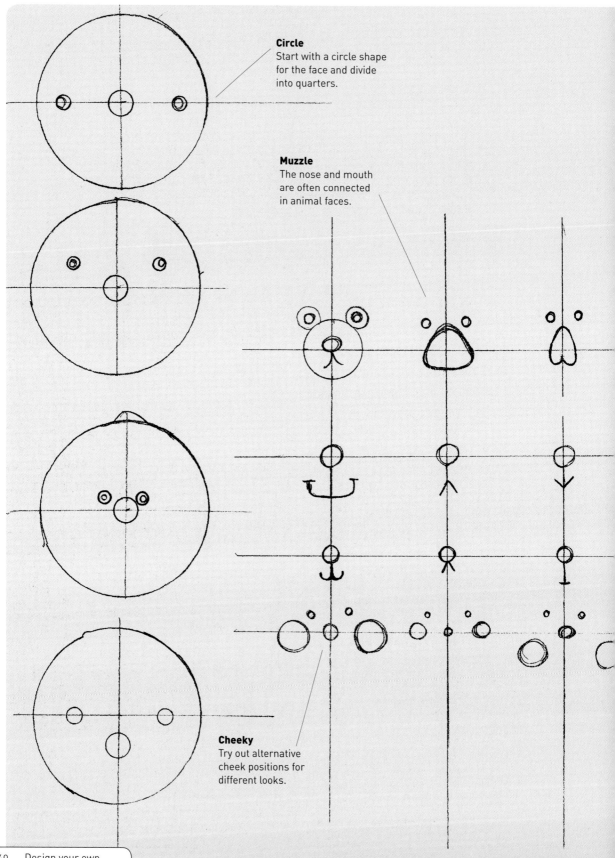

Circle
Start with a circle shape for the face and divide into quarters.

Muzzle
The nose and mouth are often connected in animal faces.

Cheeky
Try out alternative cheek positions for different looks.

Facial expressions

It is the faces of these creatures that give them such a human look, and you can change the way they look – lively or sleepy, happy or sad – with just a few lines. Look at the sketches for facial ideas to see how a simple line, or accent, can change a whole character.

It is automatic for us to draw the eyes in the top half of the face. In actual fact, for a human face, they should be placed at the halfway point between the chin and the top of the head. Divide your head into quarters. Try placing the nose on the central point, or below this line. Adding exaggerated anatomical features will help your creation to be recognizable: try a muzzle, or large ears, for instance.

This lion looks pretty serious. Turning up the corners of his mouth is easy, but try not to make him look foolish.

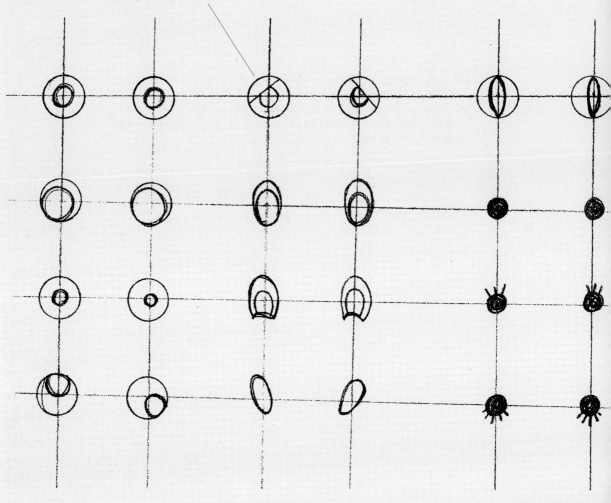

Eyelids
Droopy eyelids can look sad or tired, depending on how you draw them.

Cross-eyed
Make sure both eyes are looking in the same direction.

Eye, eye, Captain!

Making the eyes

When you look at someone's eyes, you will notice that you don't normally see the whole of the coloured part of the eye, or iris. If you draw an eye like this, it creates a very "open-eyed" effect that is almost cartoonish – ideal, perhaps, for our little amigurumi.

You'll be surprised at what a difference you can make to an expression just with the eyes. Drooping eyelids, or heavy brows, will create a world-weary look. For large and lovable eyes, make the outside large, in embroidery or with felt, and add long lashes.

Have a look at some of your favourite cartoon characters for some good ideas. Use different colours at will, but it is best to maintain the contrast between the inner and outer eye: the whites of the eye look good in white or a pale shade. Raised eyebrows will also create a certain look.

Attach bought plastic eyes with glue, unless you are around small children, when they may not be safe. Fabric, embroidery or crochet are all great alternatives.

All in favour say eye!

The eyes have it!

The menagerie

Pig

MATERIALS

2.75 mm hook
Pink yarn
Plastic eyes 7 mm (¼ in.) diameter

MEASUREMENTS

7 cm (2¾ in.) tall when piggybacked (one on top of the other)

DIRECTIONS

BODY

Make a loop with tail end of yarn on right, keeping ball end on left. Pull the ball end through loop. Make one chain through loop on hook you have drawn through to steady the circle. Dc 5 into the circle and complete with ss into the first dc.

Rnd 1: Dc 2 into each of 5 dc.
Rnd 2: * Dc 1, 2 dc into next dc * five times.
Rnd 3: * Dc 2, 2 dc into next dc * five times.
Rnd 4: * Dc 3, 2 dc into next dc * five times.
Rnd 5: * Dc 4, 2 dc into next dc * five times.
Rnds 6–12: Dc 1 all around.
Rnd 13: * Dc 4, miss 1, 1 dc * five times.
Rnd 14: Dc 1 all around.
Rnd 15: * Dc 3, miss 1, 1 dc * five times.
Rnd 16: Dc 1 all around.
Rnd 17: * Dc 2, miss 1 , 1 dc * five times.
Rnds 18–21: Dc 1 all around.
Fasten off, leaving a long tail end.

Body

NOSE

Make a loop as you did for the body, and 5 dc into the circle.

Rnd 1: Dc 2 into each of 5 dc.

Rnd 2: * Dc 1, 2 dc into next dc * five times.

Rnd 3: * Dc 2, 2 dc into next dc * five times. Fasten off.

Nose

EARS (MAKE TWO)

Ch 7, fasten off.

TAIL

Use the long ends left over when you fastened off the body to make the tail. Twist the yarn end until it doubles up on itself and makes a tiny spiral tail.

Nose
Attach the nose section to the end of the body.

Features
Position the ears and sew on. Attach the eyes with glue or make with a double French knot.

Piggyback?

Cheeky bunny

MATERIALS

3.5 mm hook
Angora in cream (for head and body)
Red wool scrap (body)
Light pink yarn scrap (nose)
Plastic eyes 7 mm (¼ in.) diameter
Red embroidery thread (for mouth)
Red felt (for cheeks) and white felt (for tiny teeth)

MEASUREMENTS

15 cm (6 in.) tall

DIRECTIONS

HEAD

Make a loop with tail end of yarn on right, keeping
ball end on left. Pull the ball end of yarn through loop.
Make one chain through loop on hook you have drawn
through to steady the circle.
Work 5 dc in to the circle and complete the circle with
ss in to the first dc.
Rnd 1: Dc 2 into each of 5 dc.
Rnd 2: * Dc 1, 2 dc into next dc * five times.
Rnd 3: * Dc 2, 2 dc into next dc * five times.
Rnds 4–7: Dc 1 into each dc.
Rnd 8: * Dc 2, miss 1, dc 1 * five times.
Rnd 9: * Dc 1, miss 1, dc 1 * five times.
Rnd 10: * Dc 1, miss 1 * repeat all around.
Fasten off.

BODY

Using red wool first, make a loop as you did for the body,
and dc 5 into the circle.
Rnd 1: Dc 2 into each of 5 dc.
Rnd 2: * Dc 1, 2 dc into next dc, * five times.
Rnd 3: * Dc 2, 2 dc into next dc * five times.
Rnd 4: * Dc 3, 2 dc into next dc * five times.
Rnds 5–7: Dc 1 all around (change the colour to cream).
Rnds 8–9: Dc 1 all around in cream, then change the
colour to red.
Rnds 10–11: Dc 1 into each dc in red.
Rnds 12–13: Dc 1 into each dc in cream.
Rnds14–15: Dc 1 all around in red then change the
colour to cream.
Add stuffing at this point.
Rnd 16: * Dc 3, miss 1, dc 1* five times.
Rnd 17: * Dc 2, miss 1, dc 1 * five times.
Rnd 18: * Dc 1, miss 1 * repeat all around.
Fasten off.

Head

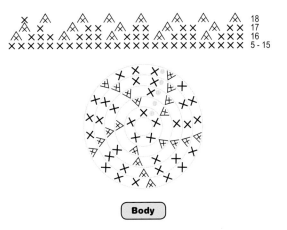

Body

MUZZLE

Using cream, make a loop as before and dc 5 into the circle.

Rnd 1: Dc 2 into each st.
Rnd 2: * Dc 1, 2 dc into next dc, * five times.
Rnd 3: * Dc 2, 2 dc into next dc, * five times.
Fasten off.

EARS (MAKE TWO)

Make 5 chains.

Rows 1–5: Ch 1, 1 dc to end.
Row 6: Dc2tog, 1 dc to last 2 st, dc2tog.
Row 7: Ch 1, 1 dc to end.
Dc 1 all around edge; fasten off.

NOSE

Using light pink yarn, make a loop as before and dc 3 into the circle.

Rnd 1: Dc 2 into each st.
Rnd 2: * Dc 1, 2 dc into next dc, * three times.
Rnd 3: Dc 1 all around.
Fasten off.

ARMS (MAKE TWO)

Using cream-coloured yarn, make a loop as before and dc 5 into the circle to start.

Rnd 1: 2 dc into each st.
Rnd 2: * Dc 1, 2 dc into next dc * five times.
Rnd 3: * Dc 2, 2 dc into next dc * five times.
Rnds 4–7: Dc 1 all around.
Rnd 8: * Dc 2, miss 1, 1 dc * five times.
Rnd 9: Dc 1 all around.
Rnd 10: Dc 1, miss 1, 1 dc * five times.
Rnds 11–12: Dc 1 all around and fasten off.
No need to stuff, make them look flappy.

LEGS (MAKE TWO)

Make these in the same way as the arms but dc 1 all around from rnds 4–10 before decreasing.

Muzzle

Arms

Ears

Nose

Rabbit's ears
Fold the ears at the base, when you sew them to the head, to create a three-dimensional ear.

Body
Dark colours near the base will balance visually.

Smile please!

Penguins

MATERIALS

2.75 mm hook
Pale blue cotton
Plastic eyes 7 mm (¼ in.) diameter
Scrap of red yarn (for hat)
Scrap of fabric (for a bib)
Orange felt (for beak)

MEASUREMENTS

7 cm (2 ¾in.) tallest

DIRECTIONS

BODY

Make a loop with tail end of yarn on right, keeping ball end on left. Pull the ball end through loop. Make one chain through loop on hook you have drawn through to steady the circle. Dc 5 into the circle and complete with ss in to the first dc.

Rnd 1: Dc 2 into each of 5 dc.
Rnd 2: * Dc 1, 2 dc into next dc * five times.
Rnd 3: * Dc 2, 2 dc into next dc * five times.
Rnd 4: * Dc 3, 2 dc into next dc * five times.
Rnd 5: * Dc 4, 2 dc into next dc * five times.

Rnds 6–10: Dc 1 all around.
Rnd 11: * Dc 4, miss 1, dc 1 * five times.
Rnd 12: Dc 1 all around.
Rnd 13: * Dc 3, miss 1, dc 1 * five times.
Rnds 14–15: Dc 1 all around.
Rnd 16: * Dc 2, miss 1, dc 1 * five times.
Rnds 17–19: Dc 1 all around.
Rnd 20: *Dc 1, miss 1, dc 1 * five times.
Rnd 21: Dc 1 all around.
Rnd 22: *Dc 1, miss 1 * five times.
Fasten off.

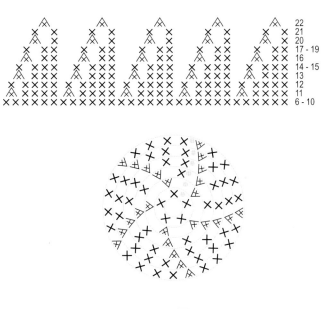

Body

TINY HAT

Make a loop as you did for the body, and 5 dc into the circle.

Rnd 1: Dc 2 into each of 5 dc.

Rnd 2: * Dc 1, 2 dc in to next dc * five times.

Rnds 3–4: Dc 1 all around.

Fasten off. Leave a long end, to make a small bobble on top of the hat.

Tiny hat

Teeny tiny hat

BABY PENGUIN

BODY

Make a loop with tail end of yarn on right, keeping ball end on left. Pull the ball end through loop. Make one chain through loop on hook you have drawn through to steady the circle. Dc 5 into the circle and complete with ss in to the first dc.

Rnd 1: 2 dc into each 5 dc.

Rnd 2: * Dc 1, 2 dc into next dc * five times.

Rnd 3: * Dc 2, 2 dc into next dc * five times.

Rnd 4: * Dc 3, 2 dc into next dc * five times.

Rnds 5–10: Dc 1 all around.

Rnd 11: * Dc 3, miss 1, * five times.

Rnd 12: Dc 1 all around.

Rnd 13: * Dc 2, miss 1, * five times.

Rnds 14–15: Dc 1 all around.

Rnds 16–17: * Dc 1, miss 1, * five times.

Fasten off.

TEENY TINY HAT

Make a loop as you did for the body, and 5 dc into the circle.

Rnd 1: Dc 2 into each 5 dc.

Rnd 2–3: Dc 1 all around.

Fasten off. Leave a long end, to make a small bobble on top of the hat.

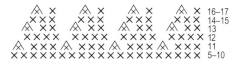

Baby body

Tiny hat
This is a French-style beret, and should be worn at a jaunty angle.

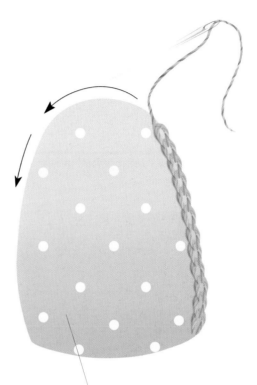

Bib
Use chain stitch to attach the bib to the body (see page 38).

Penguins

Bear

MATERIALS

3.5 mm hook
Brown yarn
Light brown yarn (for muzzle)
Red embroidery thread (for mouth)
Plastic eyes 7 mm (¼ in.) diameter

MEASUREMENTS

9 cm (3½ in.) tall

DIRECTIONS

BODY

Make a loop with tail end of yarn on right, keeping ball
end on left. Pull the ball end through loop. Make one
chain through loop on hook you have drawn through to
steady the circle. Dc 5 into the circle and complete with
ss in to the first dc.
Rnd 1: Dc 2 into each of 5 dc.
Rnd 2: * Dc 1, 2 dc into next dc * five times.
Rnd 3: * Dc 2, 2 dc into next dc * five times.
Rnd 4: * Dc 3, 2 dc into next dc * five times.
Rnds 5–7: Dc all around.
Rnd 8: * Dc 3, miss 1, 1 dc * five times.
Rnd 9: * Dc 2, miss 1, 1 dc * five times.
　　　　　Add stuffing at this point.
Rnd 10: * Dc 1, miss 1, 1 dc * five times.
Rnd 11: * Dc 1, miss 1 * five times.
Fasten off.

HEAD

Make a loop as before and 5 dc into the circle to start.
Rnd 1: Dc 2 into each of the 5 dc.
Rnd 2: * Dc 1, 2 dc into next dc * five times.
Rnd 3: * Dc 2, 2 dc into next dc * five times.
Rnd 4: * Dc 3, 2 dc into next dc * five times.
Rnds 5–9: Dc all around.
Rnd 10: * Dc 3, miss 1, 1 dc * five times.
Rnd 11: * Dc 2, miss 1, 1 dc * five times.
　　　　　Add stuffing at this point.
Rnd 12: * Dc 1, miss 1, 1 dc * five times.
Rnd 13: * Dc 1, miss 1 * five times.
Fasten off.

Body

Head

EARS (MAKE TWO)

Make a loop as before and 5 dc into the circle to start.

Rnd 1: Dc 2 into each of 5 dc.

Rnd 2: * Dc 1, 2 dc into next dc * five times.

Fasten off.

MUZZLE

With light brown yarn, make a loop as before and dc 5 into the circle to start.

Rnd 1: Dc 2 into each of 5 dc.

Rnd 2: * Dc 1, 2 dc into next dc * five times.

Fasten off.

ARMS (MAKE TWO)

Make a loop as before and dc 5 into the circle to start.

Rnd 1: Dc 2 into each st.

Rnds 2–6: Dc 1 all around.

Rnd 7: * Dc 1, miss 1 * five times.

Fasten off.

No need to stuff them.

LEGS (MAKE TWO)

Make a loop as before and dc 5 into the circle to start.

Rnd 1: Dc 2 into each st.

Rnds 2–4: Dc 1 all around.

Rnd 5: * Dc 1, miss 1 * five times.

Fasten off.

No need to stuff them.

Ears/muzzle

Arms/legs

Legs

For the legs, follow the arm chart but go straight from rows 2–4.

My jokes are unbearable

Features
Sew the muzzle onto the face and decorate with a French-knot nose and a red mouth.

Baby bear

Cocktail time!

Grumpy tiny mohair bear

MATERIALS

2.75 mm hook
Brown mohair
Dark brown yarn (for nose and mouth)
Plastic eyes 3 mm (1³⁄₁₆ in.) diameter

MEASUREMENTS

7 cm (2¾ in.) tall

DIRECTIONS

BODY

Make a loop with tail end of yarn on right, keeping ball end on left. Pull the ball end through loop.
Make one chain through loop on hook you have drawn through to steady the circle.
Work 5 dc in to the circle and complete the circle with ss into the first dc.
Rnd 1: Dc 2 into each 5 dc.
Rnd 2: * Dc 1, 2 dc into next dc * five times.
Rnds 3–7: Dc 1 all around.
Rnd 8: * Dc 1, miss 1, 1 dc * five times.
          Add stuffing at this point.
Rnd 9: Dc 1 all around.
Rnd 10: * Dc 1, miss 1 * five times.
Fasten off.

HEAD

Make a loop as before and 5 dc into the circle to start.
Rnd 1: Dc 2 into each 5 dc.
Rnd 2: * Dc 1, 2 dc into next dc * five times.
Rnd 3: * Dc 2, 2 dc into next dc * five times.
Rnds 4–5: Dc 1 all around.
Rnd 6: * Dc 2, miss 1, 1 dc * five times.
          Add stuffing at this point.
Rnd 7: * Dc 1, miss 1, 1 dc * five times.
Rnd 8: * Dc 1, miss 1 * five times.
Fasten off.

Body

Head

EARS (MAKE TWO)

Make a loop as before and dc 3 into the circle to start.

Rnd 1: 2 dc into each 3 dc.

Fasten off.

Ears

ARMS AND LEGS (MAKE FOUR)

Make a loop as before and 3 dc into the circle to start.

Rnd 1: 2 dc into each st.

Rnds 2–6: Dc 1 all around.

Rnd 7: * Dc 1, miss 1 * three times.

Fasten off; no need to stuff.

Arms/legs

I can't bear it anymore

Features
Make a nose in dark brown yarn by making 3 ch and attaching. Make a suitably down-turned mouth.

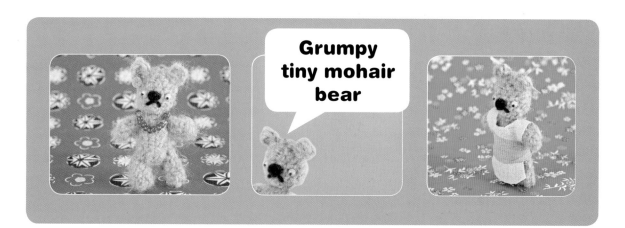

Grumpy tiny mohair bear

MATERIALS

3.5 mm hook
Dark orange and light orange acrylic yarn
Plastic eyes 10 mm (⅜ in.) diameter
Brown embroidery thread (for belly button)

MEASUREMENTS

11 cm (4½ in.) tall

DIRECTIONS

BODY

Using dark orange first: make a loop with tail end of yarn on right, keeping ball end on left. Pull the ball end through loop. Make one chain through loop on hook you have drawn through to steady the circle. Work 5 dc into the circle and complete with ss in to the first dc.

Rnd 1: Dc 2 into each 5 dc.
Rnd 2: * Dc 1, 2 dc into next dc * five times.
Rnd 3: * Dc 2, 2 dc into next dc * five times.
Rnd 4: * Dc 3, 2 dc into next dc * five times.
Rnd 5: * Dc 4, 2 dc into next dc * five times.
Rnds 6–7: Dc 1 into each st. Change to light orange.
Rnds 8–9: Dc 1 into each st, then change to dark orange.
Rnd 10: * Dc 4, miss 1 * five times.
Rnd 11: * Dc 3, miss 1 * five times. Change colour
      to light orange.
Rnd 12: * Dc 2, miss 1, 1 dc * five times.
      Add stuffing at this point.
Rnd 13: * Dc 1, miss 1, 1 dc * five times.
Rnd 14: * Dc 1, miss 1 * five times.
Fasten off.

FACE

Using dark orange first, make a loop as you did for the body, and dc 5 into the circle.

Rnd 1: Dc 2 into each of 5 dc.
Rnd 2: * Dc 1, 2 dc into next dc * five times.
Rnd 3: * Dc 2, 2 dc into next dc * five times.
Rnd 4: * Dc 3, 2 dc into next dc * five times.
Rnds 5–9: Dc 1 all around.
Rnd 10: * Dc 3, miss 1 * five times.
Rnd 11: Change the colour to light orange for the face.
      * Dc 2, miss 1, 1 dc, * five times.
      Add stuffing at this point.
Rnd 12: * Dc 1, miss 1, 1 dc * five times.
Rnd 13: Dc 1 all around.
Rnd 14: * Dc 1, miss 1 * five times.
Fasten off.

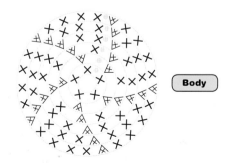

Body

Face

TAIL

Using dark orange yarn first, make a loop as before and 5 dc into the circle.

Rnd 1: Dc 2 into each st.

Rnd 2: * Dc 1, 2 dc into next st * five times.

Rnd 3: * Dc 2, 2 dc into next st * five times.

Rnd 4: * Dc 3, 2 dc into next st,* five times.

Rnds 5–8: Dc 1 into each st then change the colour to light orange.

Rnds 9–11: Dc 1 into each st then change the colour to dark orange.

Rnd 12: * Dc 3, miss 1 * five times.

Rnd 13: Dc 1 all around, then change the colour to light orange.

Rnd 14: as rnd 13.

Rnd 15: * Dc 2, miss 1, 1 dc * five times, then change the colour to dark orange.

Rnds 16–20: Dc 1 all around.

Fasten off.

Tail

EARS (MAKE TWO)

Using light orange first, make a loop as before and 5 dc into the circle to start.

Rnd 1: Dc 2 into each st.

Rnd 2: * Dc 1, 2 dc into next stitch, * five times, then change the colour to dark orange.

Rnd 3: * Dc 2, 2 dc into next stitch, * five times.

Fasten off.

EYES (MAKE TWO)

Using dark orange yarn, make a loop as before and 5 dc into the circle to start.

Rnd 1: Dc 2 into each st.

Rnd 2: * Dc 1, 2 dc into next st, * five times.

Rnd 3: * Dc 2, 2 dc into next st, * five times.

Fasten off.

Eyes/ears

ARMS (MAKE TWO)

Using dark orange yarn, make a loop as before and 5 dc into the circle to start.

Rnd 1: Dc 2 into each st.

Rnd 2: * Dc 1, 2 dc into next st, * five times.

Rnd 3: * Dc 2, 2 dc into next st, * five times.

Rnds 4–7: Dc 1 all around.

Rnd 8: * Dc 2, miss 1 * five times.

Rnd 9: Dc 1 all around.

Rnd 10: Dc 1, miss 1 * five times.

Rnds 11–12: Dc 1 all around.

Fasten off; no need to stuff.

Arms

Raccoon dog
The tanuki is a dog that has stripes like a badger or raccoon. It is a character that crops up in Japanese folklore, often as the personification of greed, hence the big belly.

Belly button
Make a large cross-stitch in the centre of the tanuki's belly. (X marks the spot.)

Heavy tail
As there are no legs, the tail is required for stability. Fill the end with plastic pellets or lentils to weigh it down.

Weights
Add Lentils

Tanuki
raccoon dog

Lion

3.5 mm hook
Rust-brown yarn (for body)
Orange and yellow yarn (for mane and tail)
Orange felt (for nose and feet)
Plastic eyes 10 mm (³⁄₈ in.) diameter
Brown embroidery thread

10 cm (4 in.) tall

DIRECTIONS

BODY

Make a loop with tail end of yarn on right, keeping ball end on left. Pull the ball end through loop. Make one chain through loop on hook you have drawn through to steady the circle.

Work 5 dc into the circle and complete the circle with ss into the first dc.

Rnd 1: Dc 2 into each 5 dc.
Rnd 2: * Dc 1, 2 dc into next dc * five times.
Rnd 3: * Dc 2, 2 dc into next dc * five times.
Rnd 4: * Dc 3, 2 dc into next dc * five times.
Rnd 5: * Dc 4, 2 dc into next dc * five times.
Rnds 6–10: Dc 1 all around.
Rnd 11: * Dc 4, miss 1, 1 dc * five times.
Rnds 12–13: Dc 1 all around.
Rnd 14: * Dc 3, miss 1, 1 dc * five times.
Rnds 15–16: Dc 1 all around.
Rnd 17: * Dc 2, miss 1, 1 dc * five times.
Rnd 18: * Dc 1, miss 1, 1 dc * five times.
Rnd 19: * Dc 1, miss 1 * five times.
Fasten off.

MANE (MAKE TWO)

Ch 36.
Row 1: * Ch 1, 5 dc into the first st, miss 1, 1 dc in next st. Repeat from * to end.
Make one with orange and one with yellow.

TAIL

Make a tiny tassel with orange yarn then attach to 18 chains in brown.

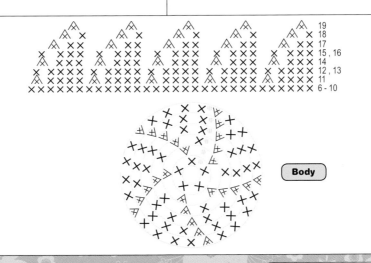

Body

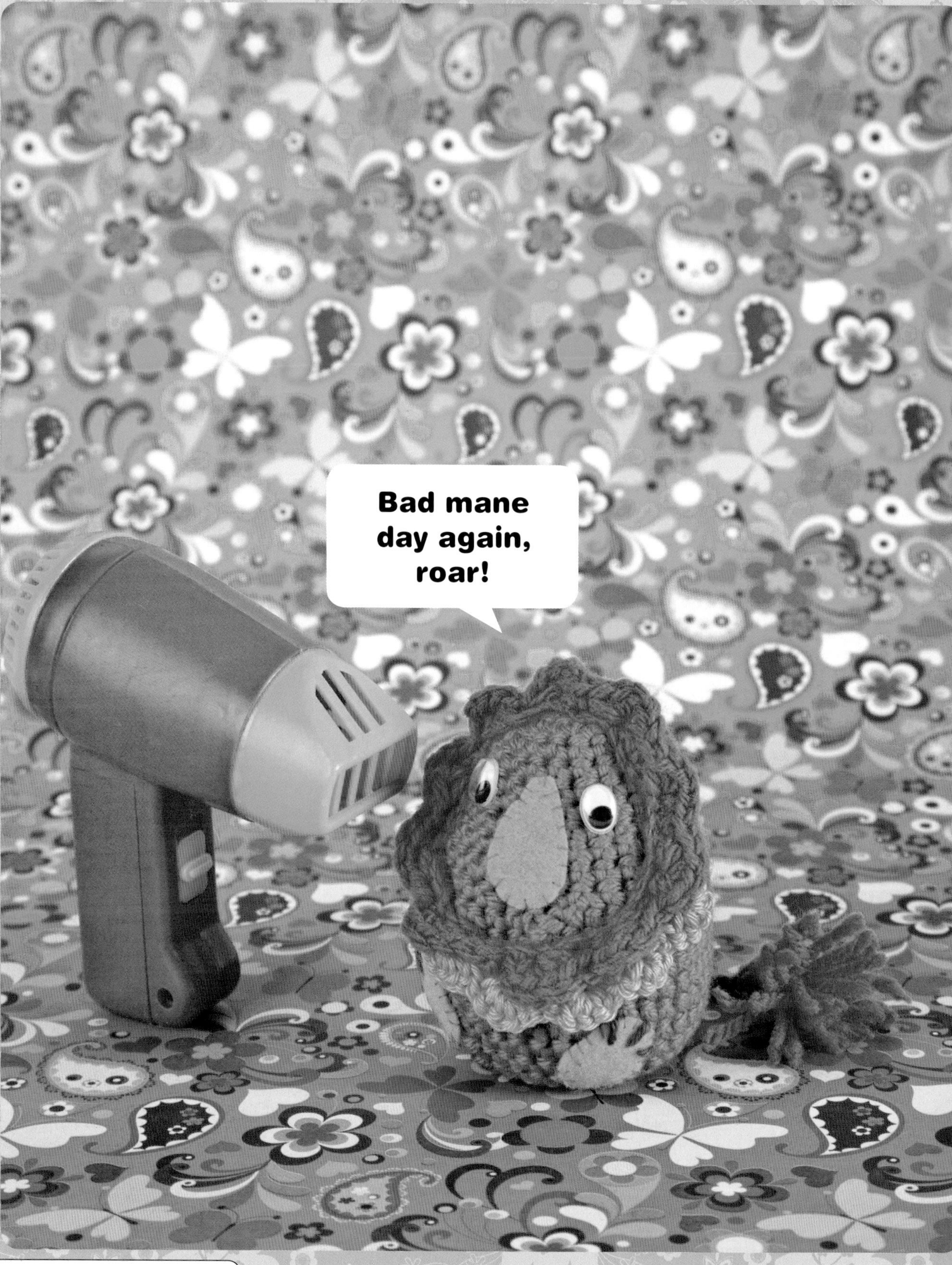
Bad mane day again, roar!

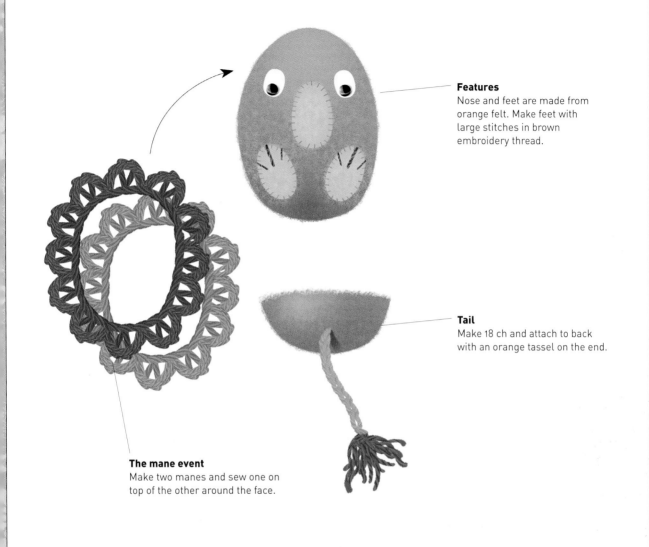

Features
Nose and feet are made from orange felt. Make feet with large stitches in brown embroidery thread.

Tail
Make 18 ch and attach to back with an orange tassel on the end.

The mane event
Make two manes and sew one on top of the other around the face.

Fierce lion

Magpies

MATERIALS

2.75 mm hook
Black yarn
Scrap of white yarn (for tummy)
Orange felt (for beak)
Plastic eyes 10 mm x 5 mm (⅜ in. x ³⁄₁₆ in.)

MEASUREMENTS

6.5 cm (2½ in.) tall

DIRECTIONS

BODY AND HEAD

Make a loop with tail end of yarn on right, keeping ball
end on left. Pull the ball end through loop. Make one
chain through loop on hook you have drawn through to
steady the circle.
Work 5 dc in to the circle and complete the circle with
ss in to the first dc.

Rnd 1: Dc 2 into each of 5 dc.
Rnd 2: * Dc 1, 2 dc into next dc * five times.
Rnd 3: * Dc 2, 2 dc into next dc * five times.
Rnd 4: * Dc 3, 2 dc into next dc * five times.
Rnds 5–9: Dc 1 all around.
Rnd 10: * Dc 3, miss 1, 1 dc * five times.
Rnd 11: * Dc 2, miss 1, 1 dc * five times.
            Add stuffing at this point.
Rnds 12–14: Dc 1 all around.
Rnd 15: * Dc 1, miss 1, 1 dc * five times.
Rnd 16: * Dc 1, miss 1 * five times.
Fasten off.

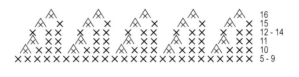

Body

TAIL

Ch 12, then join the first chain and the last one with ss.

Rnds 1–2: Dc 1 all around.

Rnd 3: * Dc 1, miss 1, repeat from * all around.

Rnd 4: Dc 1 all around.

Rnd 5: * Dc 1, miss 1, repeat from * all around until 4 sts are left.

Fasten off.

WINGS (MAKE TWO)

Ch 8.

Row 1: Ch 1, dc 1 into each of the first 2 sts, 1 tc, 1 dtr in each next 2 sts, 1 tr, 1 dc to end.

Fasten off.

1 2 3 4 5 6 7 8

Wings

Features
These plastic eyes are extra large
for the size of the face.

Tail
Sew the fat end of the tail
to the back, so that it helps
with balance. Stuff with
pellets or tufts of yarn.

Belly
Use satin stitch
to make the white
front as shown.

Magpie

Sausage dog

MATERIALS

3.5 mm hook
Brown yarn
Plastic eyes 10 mm x 5 mm (⅜ in. x ³⁄₁₆ in.)
Dark brown embroidery thread (for nose)
Red felt (for tongue)

MEASUREMENTS

16 cm (6 ⅜ in.) tall

DIRECTIONS

BODY

Make a loop with tail end of yarn on right, keeping ball end on left. Pull the ball end through loop. Make one chain through loop on hook you have drawn through to steady the circle. Work 5 dc in to the circle and complete the circle with ss in to the first dc.

Rnd 1: Dc 2 into each of 5 dc.
Rnd 2: * Dc 1, 2 dc into next dc * five times.
Rnd 3: * Dc 2, 2 dc into next dc * five times.
Rnds 4–18: Dc 1 all around.
Rnd 19: * Dc 2, miss 1, 1 dc * five times.
      Add stuffing at this point.
Rnd 20: * Dc 1, miss 1, 1 dc * five times.
Rnd 21: * Dc 1, miss 1 * five times.
Fasten off.

NECK

Using brown yarn, ch 15, join the first chain and last one with ss to form the circle.
Rnds 1–5: Dc 1 into each st.
Fasten off.

HEAD

Using brown yarn, make a loop as you did for the body, and 5 dc into the circle.
Rnd 1: Dc 2 into each of 5 dc.
Rnd 2: * Dc 1, 2 dc into next dc * five times.
Rnd 3: * Dc 2, 2 dc into next dc * five times.
Rnd 4: * Dc 3, 2 dc into next dc * five times.
Rnds 5–9: Dc 1 all around.
Rnd 10: * Dc 3, miss 1, 1 dc * five times.
Rnd 11: Dc 1 all around.
Rnd 12: * Dc 2, miss 1, 1 dc * five times.
Rnds 13–14: Dc 1 all around.
Rnd 15: * Dc 1, miss 1, 1 dc * five times.
Rnds 16–18: Dc 1 all around.
Rnd 19: * Dc 1, miss 1 * repeat all around.
Fasten off.

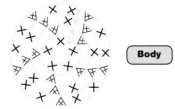

Body

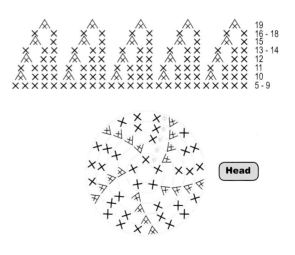

Head

FRONT LEGS (MAKE TWO)

Make a loop as before and 5 dc into the circle to start.
Rnd 1: Dc 2 into each st.
Rnd 2: * Dc 1, 2 dc into each st * five times.
Rnd 3: * Dc 2, 2 dc into each st * five times.
Rnds 4–6: Dc 1 all around.
Rnd 7: * Dc 2, miss 1, 1 dc * five times.
Rnd 8: Dc 1 all around.
Rnd 9: * Dc 1, miss 1, 1 dc * five times.
Rnd 10: * Dc 1, miss 1 * five times.
Fasten off.

Front legs

EARS (MAKE TWO)

Ch 6 to start.
Row 1: 1 ch, then 1 dc into each st to the end. Turn.
Row 2: 1 ch, then 1 dc into each st to the end. Turn.
Row 3: Dc 1 into next each 5 sts. Turn.
Rows 4–5: Ch 1, 1 dc to end. Turn.
Row 6: Dc 1 into next 4 sts. Turn.
Row 7: Ch 1, 1 dc to end.
Dc 1 all around the edge and fasten off.

TAIL (FOLD INTO HALF)

Ch 4.
Rows 1–4: Ch 1, 1 dc to end, turn.
Row 5: Dc 1 into next 3 sts.
Rows 6–8: Ch 1, 1 dc to end.
Fasten off.

Ears

Tail

BACK LEGS (MAKE TWO)

SECTION 1

Make a loop as before and 5 dc into the circle to start.
Rnd 1: Dc 2 into each st.
Rnd 2: * Dc 1, 2 dc into next st * five times.
Rnds 3–5: Dc 1 all around.
Rnd 6: *Dc 1, miss 1, 1 dc * five times.
Rnds 7–9: Dc 1 all around.
Fasten off.

Section 1

SECTION 2

Make a loop as before and 5 dc into the circle to start.
Rnd 1: Dc 2 into each st.
Rnd 2: * Dc 1, 2 dc into next st * five times.
Rnd 3: * Dc 2, 2 dc into next st * five times.
Rnds 4–6: Dc 1 all around, and fasten off.

Section 2

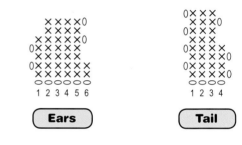

Tongue
Attach red felt tongue so it is hanging out.

Ears
Position the ears low down on the head, so that they are long and floppy.

Neck section
Attach the small ring that forms the neck to the end of the body, and fill with a little stuffing to keep his head held high.

Tail
Fold the tail section in half along its length and sew up, then sew on so that it stands up proudly.

Sausage dog

Owl

MATERIALS

3.5 mm hook
Brown yarn
Purple fine mohair (for embellishments)
White yarn (for eyes)
Plastic eyes 7 mm (¼ in.) diameter
Orange felt (for beak)

MEASUREMENTS

7 cm (2¾ in.) tall

DIRECTIONS

BODY

Make a loop with tail end of yarn on right, keeping ball end on left. Pull the ball end of yarn through loop. Make one chain through loop on hook you have drawn through to steady the circle.

Work 5 dc in to the circle and complete the circle with ss in to the first dc.

Rnd 1: Dc 2 into each of 5 dc.
Rnd 2: * Dc 1, 2 dc into next dc * five times.
Rnd 3: * Dc 2, 2 dc into next dc * five times.
Rnd 4: * Dc 3, 2 dc into next dc * five times.
Rnds 5–18: Dc 1 all around.
Fasten off.

BOTTOM

Make a circle as before, work 5 dc in to the circle and complete the circle with a ss in to the first dc.
Rnd 1: Dc 2 into each of 5 dc.
Rnd 2: * Dc 1, 2 dc into next dc * five times.
Rnd 3: * Dc 2, 2 dc into next dc * five times.
Rnd 4: * Dc 3, 2 dc into next dc * five times.
Fasten off.

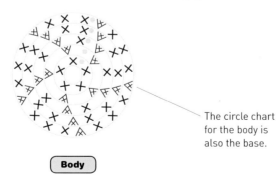

××××××××××××××××××××××××××× 5–18

The circle chart for the body is also the base.

Body

TUMMY

Using purple mohair, ch 14.

Row 1: Dc 1 into 6th ch from hook. * Ch 5, miss 3, 1 dc into next ch: rep from * to end then turn.

Row 2: * Ch 5, 1 dc into next 5 ch arch. Repeat from * to end then turn.

Repeat these 2 rows.

WINGS (MAKE TWO)

Ch 5.

Row 1: Dc 1 to end.

Row 2: Ch 1, 1 dc to last 2 st, dc2tog.

Row 3: Ch 1, 1 dc to end.

Fasten off.

Wings

EYES (MAKE TWO)

Make a loop as you did for the body, and 5 dc into the circle.

Rnd 1: Dc 2 into each of 5 dc.

Rnd 2: * Dc 1, 2 dc into next dc * five times, then change the colour to purple.

Rnd 3: * Dc 2, 2 dc into next dc * five times.

Fasten off.

Eyes

What a hoot!

Features
Sew on the eye patches and glue on plastic eyes. Sew on the belly pattern. Make a small beak out of orange felt.

Wings
Attach the wings on either side, so that they point backwards, like this.

Stuffing
Complete all the features before finishing. Insert stuffing from the base end, then sew base in place.

Owl

Monkey

MATERIALS

3.5 mm hook
Brown yarn (for body)
Light brown yarn (for face)
Plastic eyes 10 mm x 5 mm (³⁄₈ in. x ³⁄₁₆ in.)
Red embroidery thread (for mouth)
Brown embroidery thread (for nose)

MEASUREMENTS

16 cm (6³⁄₈ in.) tall

TENSION

12 st x 10 rows = 5 cm (2 in.)

DIRECTIONS

BODY

Make a loop with tail end of yarn on right, keeping ball end on left. Pull the ball end through loop. Make one chain through loop on hook you have drawn through to steady the circle. Work 5 dc in to the circle and complete the circle with ss in to the first dc.

Rnd 1: Dc 2 into each 5 dc.
Rnd 2: * Dc 1, 2 dc into next dc * five times.
Rnd 3: * Dc 2, 2 dc into next dc * five times.
Rnds 4–11: Dc 1 into each dc.
Rnd 12: * Dc 2, miss 1, dc 1 * five times.
Rnds 13–14: Dc 1 all around.
              Add stuffing at this point.
Rnd 15: * Dc 1, miss 1, dc 1 * five times.
Rnds 16–18: Dc 1 all around.
Rnd 19: Dc 1 into every other st.
Fasten off.

FACE

Make a loop as you did for the body, and 5 dc into the circle.

Rnd 1: Dc 2 into each 5 dc.
Rnd 2: * Dc 1, 2 dc in to next dc * five times.
Rnd 3: * Dc 2, 2 dc in to next dc * five times.
Rnd 4: * Dc 3, 2 dc in to next dc * five times.
Rnds 5–9: Dc 1 all around.
Rnd 10: * Dc 3, miss 1, 1 dc * five times.
              Change the colour to light brown for the face.
Rnd 11: * Dc 2, miss 1, 1 dc * five times.
              Add stuffing at this point.
Rnd 12: * Dc 1, miss 1, 1 dc * five times.
Rnd 13: * Dc 1, miss 1 * five times.
Fasten off.

Body

Face

MUZZLE

Using light brown yarn, make a loop as before and 5 dc into the circle.

Rnd 1: Dc 2 into each st.

Rnd 2: * Dc 1, 2 dc into next st * five times.

Rnd 3: * Dc 2, 2 dc into next st * five times.

Rnds 4–6: Dc 1 around.

Rnd 7–8: * Dc 1, miss 1 * all around.

Fasten off.

EARS (MAKE TWO)

Make a loop as before and 5 dc into the circle to start. Start with the light brown yarn

Rnd 1: Dc 2 into each of 5 dc , then change the colour to brown yarn.

Rnd 2: * Dc 1, 2 dc into next dc * five times.

Fasten off.

ARMS (MAKE TWO)

Using brown yarn, make a loop as before and dc 5 into the circle to start.

Rnd 1: Dc 2 into each st.

Rnd 2: * Dc 1, 2 dc into next st * five times.

Rnd 3: * Dc 2, 2 dc into next st * five times.

Rnds 4–10: Dc 1 all around.

Rnd 11: * Dc 2, miss 1, dc 1 * five times.

Rnd 12: * Dc 1, miss 1, dc 1 * five times.
Add stuffing at this point.

Rnd 13: * Dc 1, miss 1 * five times.

Fasten off.

LEGS (MAKE TWO)

Make these in the same way as making the arms, but dc 1 all around from rnds 4–7 before decreasing.

Ears

Arms/legs

Muzzle

Features
Attach the muzzle with a little stuffing to make it stand out. Make a big smile with red yarn and chain stitch.

Monkey see, monkey do

Panda bear

MATERIALS

3.5 mm hook
Black and white acrylic yarns
Plastic eyes 10 mm x 5 mm (³⁄₈ in. x ³⁄₁₆ in.)
Red embroidery thread (for mouth)

MEASUREMENTS

16 cm (6³⁄₈ in.) tall

DIRECTIONS

BODY

Using black yarn, make a loop as before and 5 dc into the circle.

Rnd 1: Dc 2 into each of 5 dc.

Rnd 2: * Dc 1, 2 dc into next dc * five times.

Rnd 3: * Dc 2, 2 dc into next dc * five times.

Rnd 4: * Dc 3, 2 dc into next dc * five times.

Rnds 5–7: Dc 1 around (change the colour to white).

Rnds 8–9: Dc 1 around in white, then change to black.

Rnds 10–11: Dc 1 around in black.

Rnds 12–13 : Dc 1 around in white.

Rnds14–15: Dc 1 around in white, then change to black yarn. Add stuffing at this point.

Rnd 16: * Dc 3, miss 1, 1 dc * five times.

Rnd 17: * Dc 2, miss 1 , 1 dc * five times, 1 dc.

Rnd 18: * Dc 1, miss 1 * all around.

Fasten off.

HEAD

Make a loop with tail end of yarn on right, keeping ball end on left. Pull the ball end through loop. Make one chain through loop on hook you have drawn through to steady the circle. Work 5 dc in to the circle and complete the circle with ss in to the first dc.

Rnd 1: Dc 2 into each of 5 dc.

Rnd 2: * Dc 1, 2 dc into next dc * five times.

Rnd 3: * Dc 2, 2 dc into next dc * five times.

Rnds 4–7: Dc 1 all around.

Rnd 8: * Dc 2, miss 1, 1 dc * five times.

Rnd 9: * Dc 1, miss 1, 1 dc * five times.

Rnd 10: Dc 1 into every alternate st.

Fasten off.

Body

Head

NOSE

Using black yarn, make a loop as before and 5 dc into the circle.

Rnd 1: Dc 2 into each st.
Rnd 2: * Dc 1, 2 dc into next dc * five times.
Rnd 3: * Dc 2, 2 dc into next dc * five times.
Rnd 4: * Dc 2, miss 1 * five times.
Fasten off.

EYES (MAKE 2)

Using black yarn, make a loop as before and 3 dc into the circle.

Rnd 1: 2 dc into each st.
Rnd 2: * Dc 1, 2 dc into each st * three times.
Rnd 3: Dc 1 into next 4 st.
Row 4: Turn without making ch, 1 dc into next 3 dc.
Row 5: Turn with 1 ch, 1 dc into next 3 dc.
Fasten off.

EARS (MAKE 2)

Using black yarn, make a loop as before and 3 dc into the circle.

Rnd 1: Dc 2 into each st.
Rnd 2: * Dc 1, 2 dc into next st * three times.
Rnd 3: * Dc 2, 2 dc into next st * three times.
Rnd 4: * Dc 3, 2 dc into next st * three times.
Fasten off.

ARMS AND LEGS (MAKE 4)

Using black, make a loop as before and 5 dc into the circle to start.

Rnd 1: Dc 2 into each st.
Rnd 2: * Dc 1, 2 dc into next st * five times.
Rnd 3: * Dc 2, 2 dc into next st * five times.
Rnds 4–10: Dc 1 all around.
Rnd 11: * Dc 2, miss 1, dc 1 * five times.
    Add stuffing at this point.
Rnd 12: * Dc 1, miss 1, dc 1 * five times.
Rnd 13: * Dc 1, miss 1 * five times.
Fasten off.

Nose

Eyes

Ears

Arms

Features
Sew on nose and eye patches.
Glue on plastic eyes and make
a chain-stitch mouth in red yarn.

Superhero Panda

Field mouse

MATERIALS

2.75 mm hook
White mohair
Scrap of pink yarn (for nose)
Plastic eyes 3 mm (⅛ in.) diameter
Cream felt (for ears and cheeks)

MEASUREMENTS

6 cm (2¼ in.) tall

DIRECTIONS

BODY

Make a loop with tail end of yarn on right, keeping ball end on left. Pull the ball end through loop.
Make one chain through loop on hook you have drawn through to steady the circle. Work 5 dc in to the circle and complete the circle with ss in to the first dc.

(Body)

Rnd 1: Dc 2 into each 5 dc.
Rnd 2: * Dc 1, 2 dc into next dc * five times.
Rnd 3: * Dc 2, 2 dc into next dc, * five times.
Rnds 4–10: Dc 1 all around.
Rnd 11: * Dc 2, miss 1, dc 1 * five times.
    Add the stuffing at this point.
Rnd 12: * Dc 1, miss 1, dc 1 * five times.
Rnd 13: * Dc 1, miss 1 * five times.
Fasten off.

NOSE

Make a loop as you did for the body, and 5 dc in to the circle.
Rnd 1: Dc 2 into each 5 dc.
Rnds 2–3: Dc 1 all around.
Fasten off.

EARS (MAKE TWO)

Make 18 chains, join the first chain and the last chain with ss, to form the circle.
Dc 15 all around the circle. Fasten off.

FINISHING   sew together following the diagram

Ears
Make double crochet stitches around the chain.

Felt ears
Sew felt shapes to the back of the chain ears.

Features
Sew on the nose and make cheeks out of felt.

Skinny sleepy cat

MATERIALS

2.75 mm hook
White angora
Light grey yarn (for muzzle, ears, legs
and arms)
Red embroidery thread (for mouth)
Brown embroidery thread (for eyes)

MEASUREMENTS

10 cm (4 in.) tall

DIRECTIONS

BODY

Make a loop with tail end of yarn on right, keeping ball
end on left. Pull the ball end through loop.

Make one chain through loop on hook you have drawn
through to steady the circle. Work 5 dc in to the circle
and complete the circle with ss in to the first dc.

Rnd 1: Dc 2 into each of 5 dc.

Rnd 2: * Dc 1, 2 dc into next dc * five times.

Rnd 3: * Dc 2, 2 dc into next dc * five times.

Rnds 4–10: Dc 1 all around.

Rnd 11: * Dc 2, miss 1, dc 1 * five times.

Rnd 12: Dc 1 all around.

Rnds 13–14: * Dc 1, miss 1 * five times.

Fasten off.

HEAD

Make a loop as before and 5 dc into the circle to start.

Rnd 1: Dc 2 into each 5 dc.

Rnd 2: * Dc 1, 2 dc into next dc * five times.

Rnd 3: * Dc 2, 2 dc into next dc * five times.

Rnd 4: * Dc 3, 2 dc into next dc * five times.

Rnds 5–9: Dc 1 all around.

Rnd 10: * Dc 3, miss 1, dc 1 * five times.

Rnd 11: * Dc 2, miss 1, dc 1 * five times.

        Add stuffing at this point.

Rnd 12: * Dc 1, miss 1, dc 1 * five times.

Rnd 13: * Dc 1, miss 1 * five times.

Fasten off.

Body

Head

EARS (MAKE TWO)

With light grey yarn, ch 4.
Row 1: Ch 1, dc 1 to end.
Row 2: Dc 1 into next 3 st.
Row 3: Dc 1 into next 2 st.
Fasten off.

MUZZLE

With light brown yarn, make a loop as before and dc 5 into the circle to start.
Rnd 1: Dc 2 into each of 5 dc.
Rnd 2: * Dc 1, 2 dc into next dc * five times.
Fasten off.

Muzzle

1 2 3 4

Ears

ARMS AND LEGS (MAKE FOUR)

Make a loop as before and 5 dc into the circle to start.
Rnd 1: Dc 2 into each st.
Rnds 2–6: Dc 1 all around.
Rnd 7: * Dc 1, miss 1 * five times.
Fasten off; no need to stuff.

2 - 6

Arms / legs

Yawn!!
Time for a catnap.

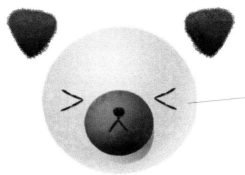

Features
Sew on the muzzle and ears. Make slits for closed eyes with yarn, and a mouth to match. The nose is a French knot in brown yarn.

Arms and legs
Attach the head and limbs in the appropriate places.

Skinny sleepy cat

Elephant

MATERIALS

3.5 mm hook
Blue yarn
Red embroidery thread (for mouth)
Plastic eyes 7 mm (¼ in.) diameter

MEASUREMENTS

10 cm (4 in.) tall

DIRECTIONS

BODY

Make a loop with tail end of yarn on right, keeping ball end on left. Pull the ball end through loop. Make one chain through loop on hook you have drawn through to steady the circle. Work 5 dc in to the circle and complete the circle with ss in the first dc.

Rnd 1: Dc 2 into each of 5 dc.
Rnd 2: * Dc 1, 2 dc into next dc * five times.
Rnd 3: * Dc 2, 2 dc into next dc * five times.
Rnd 4: * Dc 3, 2 dc into next dc * five times.
Rnds 5–9: Dc 1 all around.
Rnd 10: * Dc 3, miss 1, 1 dc * five times.
Rnd 11: * Dc 2, miss 1 * five times.
        Add the stuffing at this point.
Rnd 12: * Dc 1, miss 1 st, 1 dc * five times.
Rnd 13: * Dc 1, miss 1 st, * five times.
Fasten off.

HEAD

Make a loop as before and 5 dc into the circle to start.
Rnd 1: Dc 2 into each of 5 dc.
Rnd 2: * Dc 1, 2 dc into next dc * five times.
Rnd 3: * Dc 2, 2 dc into next dc * five times.
Rnd 4: * Dc 3, 2 dc into next dc * five times.
Rnds 5–9: Dc 1 all around.
Rnd 10: * Dc 3, miss 1st, 1 dc * five times.
Rnd 11: * Dc 2, miss 1st, 1 dc * five times.
        Add the stuffing at this point.
Rnd 12: * Dc 1, miss 1, 1 dc * five times.
Rnd 13: * Dc 1, miss 1 * five times.
Rnds 14–20: Dc 1 all around (for trunk).

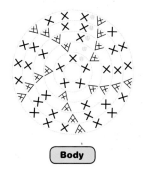

Body

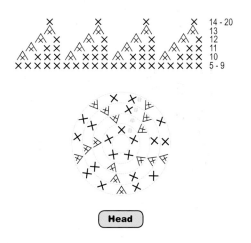

Head

EARS (MAKE TWO)

Make a loop as before and dc 5 into the circle to start.

Rnd 1: Dc 2 into each of 5 dc.

Rnd 2: * Dc 1, 2 dc into next dc * five times.

Rnd 3: * Dc 2, 2 dc into next dc * five times.

Fasten off.

ARMS (MAKE TWO)

Make a loop as before and dc 5 into the circle to start.

Rnd 1: Dc 2 into each st.

Rnd 2: * Dc 1, 2 dc into next dc * five times.

Rnds 3–4: Dc 1 all around.

Rnd 5: * Dc 1, miss 1, * five times.

Rnds 6–7: Dc 1 all around.

Rnd 8: * Dc 1, miss 1 * five times.

Fasten off. No need to stuff.

LEGS (MAKE TWO)

Make a loop as before and 5 dc into the circle to start.

Rnd 1: Dc 2 into each st.

Rnd 2: * Dc 1, 2 dc into next dc * five times.

Rnds 3–7: Dc 1 all around.

Add stuffing, and fasten off.

(Legs)

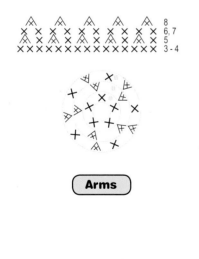

(Ears)

(Arms)

Features
Make sure the trunk is stuffed firmly so that it doesn't droop. Add ears, eyes and a chain stitch mouth in red.

Limbs
Add all the arms and legs in the appropriate places.

Let's play

Amigurumi Gallery

The Internet has served to make the crafting world ever smaller, and more fertile, keeping new ideas travelling, and growing, fast. It also works as a support network, with makers able to gain feedback on their work, as well as selling their wares to a wide audience. Group sites mean small crafters can afford to make a blog, or display their work in a way that would have been impossible a few years ago.

The increased use of diagrams and charts also means that patterns are translated more easily than in the past. Japanese craft books have a different aesthetic to work you can see in America or Europe. Their clear and novel style is sought-after in the West, and buying Japanese craft books has become the latest expensive pastime for serious crafters. Try searching for amigurumi on the web: here is a small selection of makers that we liked the look of.

Name: Niji aka Irisgurumi
Website: www.irisgurumi.com
A little about me... My name is Niji, I'm Thai, originally from Bangkok. Now I'm living in Alicante, Spain. In February 2007 I started my very first amigurumi – I had never touched a crochet hook before. Now, I can say that I love amigurumi.

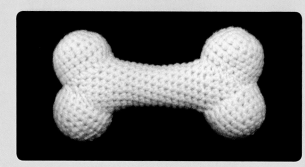

Name: Cynthia Rae
Website: www.candypopcreations.etsy.com
A little about me... Working in Iowa, USA, Cynthia Rae is a textile artist in a permanent state of inspiration, designing original patterns that bring a unique, contemporary flare to classic fibre art.

Name: MUFFA aka Mariella's
Unusual Fantasy Funny Animals
Website: www.muffa.bravehost.com
A little about me... I live in
sunny Italy and love to create
miniature animals. My mother and
grandmother taught me to knit,
crochet and embroider and I have
been doing crafts ever since!
I have a passion for all things small,
mini, micro and sweet. I surprise
myself "giving life" to micro
animals, bears, and fairies.
I usually work with a 0.50 mm hook
– someday I'll go blind!

Name: Emily Miller aka Crochet Obsession
Website: www.crochetobsession.blogspot.com
A little about me... I live in Phoenix, Arizona,
USA, with my husband and two children.
I have been crocheting since I was 12,
and for a long time I only made blankets.
A combination of Mr Rogers, and my four-year-
old got me back into crocheting after a long
pause. Mr Rogers had a show where he visited a
friend that made animals: my son loved the idea
of having me make him an animal. What child
wouldn't want their very own live-in toy maker?
So my crochet obsession was reborn.

Name: Marci Senders
Website: www.marcisenders.com
A little about me... I am a Senior Designer
for Random House Books for Young
Readers. Other than crocheting in my
spare time, I like to illustrate, collage
and alter books.

Name: Samantha Wilson
Website: www.eureekaswindow.etsy.com
A little about me... A college student in Connecticut, USA, with an addiction to crafts, especially crocheting and sewing, I create my own amigurumi patterns based on random inspirations and things that I love.

Name: Ruby Submarine
Website: www.rubysubmarine.
blogspot.com
A little about me... I currently live in Culver City, California, USA, I have been crafting since my grandmother taught me to knit when I was four. I am self-taught at crochet, have no idea how to use patterns and free-form crochet everything I make. My favourite things to make are sea creatures, hats and fake food (especially good for fake food fights).

Name: Hansigurumi aka Hansi Singh
Website: www.hansigurumi.etsy.com
A little about me... Hansigurumi, who is merely Hansi in her everyday life, credits her son Ambrose for inspiring a love of knitted toys and other peculiarities. She lives with Ambrose and her partner Aaron in Seattle, Washington, USA.

Name: Jenifer Spangenberg aka Truly Outrageous
Website: www.TrulyOutrageous.etsy.com
A little about me... I am from Cherry Hill, New Jersey, USA.

Name: Ana Paula Rimoli
Website: www.anapaulaoli.etsy.com
A little about me... Hola! My children are the inspiration for all the toys I make. I love, love, love crocheting and making toys. I've been making stuff for as long as I can remember and I have to thank my neighbour Martita in Montevideo for teaching me how to crochet when I was little, I think six or seven, sitting outside one summer.

Name: My4heads aka Paulette Morrissey
Website: www.13sites.com
A little about me... Born and raised in Wisconsin, USA – by day, I'm an artist, working in coloured pencils, watercolours and ink. In the evenings, I like designing little crochet creatures and patterns.

Name: Donielle Martin aka turtle kisses
Website: www.turtlekisses.com
A little about me... Donielle is a wife
and mother of three living in Minnesota,
USA, currently working as security for a
clothing store, but greatly enjoys making
amigurumi in her spare time.

Name: PlanetJune aka June Gilbank
Website: www.planetjune.com
A little about me... June designs original
crochet patterns for cute amigurumi
softies, and runs the PlanetJune craft
blog from Ontario, Canada.

Name: Leanne Poon aka t0fugurl
Website: www.t0fugurl.etsy.com
A little about me... I live in Vancouver, Canada, and I only started crocheting last summer. I had a preconception that crocheting was so "grandma", but I'm glad I learned how to make amigurumi and I've been hooked ever since.

Name: Eternal Sunshine aka Alicia Kachmar
Website: www.aliciakachmar.com
A little about me... I originally hail from Pittsburgh, PA, but currently live in Brooklyn, NY, USA. I'm a Jill-of-all-trades so to speak: a museum educator/teacher turned freelance writer/crafter/DIYer, and I love to cook and bake, bike-ride and explore.

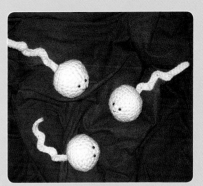

Name: Jenni Love
Website: www.theselovinghands.etsy.com
A little about me... Living in Ontario, Canada, I am a mother of two wonderful boys. After crocheting for ten years, my sister introduced me to amigurumi and I got hooked. I now crochet my own original creatures and write patterns.

Name: Shelley Becking
Website: www.thehookery.etsy.com
A little about me... I live in Ottawa, Ontario, Canada. I took up crochet about a year ago while on maternity leave from my full-time job. My children and their imagination inspire most of my projects. I started to crochet My Pet Monster for my three-year-old and now I can't stop! I never know what Monster will be born until I'm done. They are OOAK (one of a kind).

Name: Wren Yu aka love yu critters
Website: www.loveyu.etsy.com
A little about me... I am a self-taught crafter who
lives, loves, and crochets in Atlanta, Georgia, USA.

Name: Nelly Pailloux aka La Fée Crochette
Website: www.lafeecrochette.
blogspot.com
A little about me... I'm French and totally
addicted to creating tiny little creatures
in my small workshop in the English
countryside. I find inspiration in cookery
books and children's illustrations.

Name: Andrea Onishi aka Lacrafi
Website: www.lacrafiteira.etsy.com
www.superziper.blogspot.com (my craft
blog in Portuguese)
A little about me... I craft at my small
studio in São Paulo, Brazil. I crochet,
knit, sew and draw. My creative name
is Lacrafi (short for Lacrafiteira.) I love
making amigurumi because it is one
of the most creative handicrafts. With
pieces of yarn and crochet needles I feel
free to create the most amazing objects.

Name: Trinlay Khadro
Website: www.trinlayk.etsy.com
A little about me... I'm a long-time artist and crafter making my art and crafting my "real job", while learning how to live with illness and disability. I live with my almost grown-up daughter and two cats. I've discovered etsy via flickr, and hope it will be as much fun.

Name: Erin Nicholson aka squirrel of snooze
Website: www. squirrelofsnooze.etsy.com
A little about me...
Erin Nicholson is a Vancouver-based designer and artist, who would likely have never taken up crochet had it not been for the recent crafts revival and crafting community online.

Name: Julie King aka Gleefulthings
Website: www.gleefulthings.com
A little about me... I'm 24 and live in southern
California. I have always loved making things!
I learned how to crochet about three years ago
and have been addicted ever since. About a year ago,
I started my business Gleeful Things as a place to
sell crocheted toys that I design, as well as crochet
patterns that I've written.

Name: Amy Lin
Website: www.melbangel.etsy.com
A little about me... I am a stay-at-home mum from Singapore. I started crafting as a hobby. Then I found the "Etsy" site for handmade products. I became an online seller there. I mainly sell crochet patterns, which are all my original creations, and also some unique crocheted finished products. My customers come from many countries including the USA, UK, Australia, Malaysia, France, Sweden, and Thailand.

Name: Amy Gaines
Website: www.amygaines.etsy.com
A little about me... I am a stay-at-home mother, living in Massachusetts, USA, from where I operate my online pattern shop.

Name: Kim Yeoh
Website: www.kqcreative.com
A little about me... I am a handicraft hobbyist living in Singapore.

Name: Crochet Accessory
Website: www.crochetaccessory.com
A little about us... We are two sisters, both professional business women – one based in Shanghai and the other in New York – who share a fondness for unique crocheted artworks, especially amigurumi. We started our business of making and selling amigurumi about two years ago and hope to share our passion for amigurumi with a broader audience.

Name: Michelle
Website: www.chezmichelle.etsy.com
www.stores.ebay.com/Suncatchers-Eyes
A little about me... I started out designing crochet patterns – meet Little Emo – now my business has switched gears. I could never find the colours and sizes of acrylic safety eyes that I wanted, so I started painting my own. Now I sell Suncatcher Eyes on Etsy and Ebay.

Name: Kim Werker
Website: www.kimwerker.com
A little about me... I am the editor of
Interweave Crochet magazine and the
founder of CrochetMe.com; I live in
Vancouver, BC, Canada.

Name: Helena Shimizu
aka kawaiikewpie
Website: www.
kawaiikewpie.com
A little about me...
I am a production artist
working in a marketing
agency in Los Angeles,
USA. During my freetime
I enjoy handicrafts like
amigurumi, drawing
and sewing by hand.
I also collect, swap,
and sell anything *kawaii*,
Japanese for cute.

Name: Raewa dolly
Website: www.raewadolly.etsy.com
A little about me... Hello from
Bangkok, Thailand. My sister and
I love dolls. So, we thought that
there are many people (not only
kids) that love dolls and want to
have a good collection of them
– that's why we started RaewaDolly.
You will see lots of dolls and cute
stuff in our shop.

Name: Yuka Yamaguchi
Website: www.plastiquemonkey.com
A little about me... I was born in
Kobe, Japan and am now living in
Saskatoon, Canada. I've recently
started telling people I'm an artist.
I'm self-taught. I make useless toys
and art for adult children. My ongoing
project is the "turn everything around
you cute and fun project."

Resources

The joy of knitting small is that you don't always need to rush out and buy a load of expensive yarn. However, should your amigurumi habit get out of hand, there are plenty of retailers that can help. Here are a few tried and tested suppliers that you can find on the internet and probably in your local yarn shop.

ONLINE YARN STORES

www.angelyarns.com/
www.laughinghens.com
www.masonsneedlecraft.co.uk
www.woolworks.org
www.knitshop.co.uk
www.knitandsew.co.uk
www.prickyourfinger.com
www.loop.gb.com
www.debbieblissonline.com
www.iknit.org.uk
www.knitrowan.com

OUR LOCAL KNITTING SHOPS

Prick Your Finger
260 Globe Road
Bethnal Green
London E2 0JD

Loop
41 Cross Street
Islington, London
N1 2BB

I Knit
13 Bonnington Square
Vauxhall
London SW8 1TE

Lenarow
169 Blackstock Road
London N4 2JS

YARN SUPPLIERS

Berroco, Inc.
www.berroco.com

Blue Sky Alpacas, Inc
www.blueskyalpacas.com

Crystal Palace yarns
www.straw.com

Designer Yarns
www.designeryarns.uk.com

Koigu Wool Designs
www.koigu.com

Lion Brand Yarns
www.lionbrand.com

Manos del Uruguay
www.rosiesyarncellar.com

Misti Alpaca
www.mistialpaca.com

GGH
www.muenchyarns.com

Patons
www.patonsyarns.com

Plymouth Yarn Co.
www.plymouthyarn.com

HOOKS

Brittany
www.brittanyneedles.com

Clover
www.clover-usa.com

Pony
www.pony-needles.com

Turn of the Century
www.turn2001.com

Right: You will never guess whose these intrepid robbers are. They have made a haul and are making good their escape.

Index